THE
SWINDON & CRICKLADE RAILWAY

and former Midland & South Western Junction Railway lines

• A PAST AND PRESENT COMPANION •

A nostalgic trip along the former M&SWJR route from Andoversford to Marlborough

John Stretton

2nd-SINGLE SINGLE-2nd
Swindon Junction to
Swindon Jn. Swindon Jn
Cricklade Cricklade
CRICKLADE
Via L'p Line & Swinden Tn
(W) 1/10 Fare 1/10 (W)
For conditions see over For conditions see over
1044 1044

• RAILWAY HERITAGE •
from
The NOSTALGIA Collection

First published in 2003

British Library Cataloguing in Publication Data

A catalogue record for this book is available from the British Library.

ISBN 1 85895 218 2

Past & Present Publishing Ltd
The Trundle
Ringstead Road
Great Addington
Kettering
Northants NN14 4BW

Tel/Fax: 01536 330588
email: sales@nostalgiacollection.com
Website: www.nostalgiacollection.com

Printed and bound in Great Britain

Past and Present

A Past & Present book
from
The NOSTALGIA *Collection*

ACKNOWLEDGEMENTS

There are too many to list everyone who has contributed to the end product, but they know who they are and they are hereby thanked, even if their name does not appear. Among those who deserve especial mention are: Neville Bridger, Dennis Compton (Area Manager Wiltshire County Council, Enviromental Services), John Edgington, Reg Palk, Jim Larkin, Hugh Ballantyne, Paul Chancellor, Richard Casserley, Colin Caddy, Terry Gough, Frank Hornby, Jim Clarke, Mike Esau, John Spencer Gilks, and Cliff Vaisey. In addition, Peter, Mick and Will at Silver Link Publishing have been their usual towers of strength; and Judi, my wife, has borne with the long gestation of this book, especially when she wanted my help and attention with other things, such as Christmas! Thank you all – without you…

CONTENTS

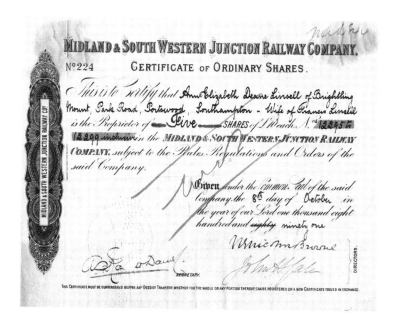

A wonderful evocation of the atmosphere of the line covered by this book. While M&SWJR services ran from Cheltenham to Southampton, our focus begins at Andoversford Junction, where the Southampton trains branched southwards, leaving the GWR Cheltenham-Kingham-Banbury/Oxford route to continue eastwards. On 7 September 1955 No 6387 coasts past the 1935-vintage, standard GWR signal box and into the junction station, plenty of steam in hand, at the head of the 2.00pm train from Cheltenham St James to Southampton. A Swindon locomotive at the time, No 6387 would move to Banbury shed two months after this view. *Hugh Ballantyne*

INTRODUCTION

Without doubt this has been the hardest 'Past and Present' title on which I have worked! The reason? Obliteration. While in previous books – and, indeed, in so many areas of past railway operation – there have been identifiable landmarks, railway architecture or, say, boundary fences and/or markings, neighbouring buildings, this has not been the case for around 90 per cent of the locations covered in this latest volume. This has led to distinct problems on the ground, greater detective work and frustration, and disappointment mixed with the thrill of the challenge. Additionally, this project has been far more isolated for me than of yore, with fewer contacts with the general public in the 'present' photographic research. However, those who have been approached, or who were in turn 'nosey', have been universally fascinated, delighted and genuinely pleased with both the project itself and the anticipation at the finished product. I hope I will not have disappointed them! Many decried the very obliteration that I was witnessing, lamenting the disappearance of the sights in the 'past' photographs and echoing the widespread opinion that the wholesale destruction of so much of our railway infrastructure was both criminal and short-sighted. To quote one resident of Marlborough, 'We need the railway now to get to Swindon. The roads are death traps; but we cannot put them back as the sites have been built on.' Amen. Fortunately, through the good offices of the Swindon & Cricklade Railway, at least a part of the ex-M&SWJR is being reborn with rails on it!

The main body of the book looks at the heritage bequeathed to the preservationists, travelling down the line from Andoversford to Marlborough, comparing the present with the past and incorporating appropriate details in the extended captions. The final section is given over to the S&CR, its progress and some of its restoration programmes. A Gazetteer and Index complete the menu. In common with all the books on which I have worked, this has been a fascinating project from which I have learned a great deal. If for no other reason, this factor has made the work pleasurable. I feel far more understanding of the background to the railway, its operations and the localities through which it ran. I only hope that the reader will assimilate some of this for themselves and that they will also enjoy the illustrations contained herein. For me, the sheer disparity between the 'then' and 'now' has its own wonder, in addition to glimpsing just some of the delights that are now denied us. In addition, the views of the progress of the preservationists, often against seemingly mountainous odds, are both impressive and humbling. Those of us who are 'armchair' supporters owe a massive debt of gratitude to all those who get their hands dirty.

In addition, I have been told many stories about the railways past and present, some amusing and all fascinating and entertaining in their turn. Reg Palk's father worked on the former M&SWJR south of Swindon Town, during and after the Second World War. On one occasion during the war, while at Marlborough, an American Army Jeep roared into the station yard, screeching to a halt. A Sergeant jumped out, yelling that he wanted an Engineer. Reg's father responded and was hastily ushered into the Jeep, which then proceeded to roar at breakneck speed to Savernake, ignoring speed limits, road conditions and other road users. There, an ambulance train, carrying seriously injured American servicemen back from fighting in Europe, was stopped with a 'hot' coach axlebox. Still somewhat shaken by the ride, Palk Snr attended to the problem and eventually the train restarted its journey. In gratitude, the Sergeant offered him a ride back to Marlborough, but nerves got the upper hand and he politely declined, preferring to travel back in the cab of the next up goods train! A year or two later he was again working at Savernake, in the sidings, when a wagon in a train of spent munitions caught fire. Fortunately he was not too close to it at the time, but needless to say he and several colleagues scattered at the noises and pieces of flying metal and quickly took cover under an empty wagon!

I have acknowledged elsewhere many of those who have helped this project come to fruition, but I would just like to repeat here my gratitude for each and every one of them, their ready, courteous and sympathetic help and encouragement, in whatever way they became involved. They have all added to the sum total of this book and I hope that the reader derives as much enjoyment from it as I have had in putting it together.

The M&SWJR had a wide catalogue of endemic locomotives, large and small, tank and tender, and many were truly stylish designs. In original condition, complete with smart lined red livery, M&SWJR No 4 (*top*) elegantly looks the part as it stands on the railway's Andover Junction shed turntable on 30 April 1921. Together with sister locomotive No 31, ordered at the same time, it differed from the existing trio of this design of 4-4-0s in having two

domes, the rear one containing a top feed for the boiler and surmounted with Ross 'pop' safety valves. The Class, mostly based at Cheltenham, were the pride of the line, steaming freely and having an enviable reliability record. Note the tender coal rails; these were later replaced with solid sheets. Assimilated into the GWR fleet at the Grouping of 1923, it was renumbered 1122 and withdrawn in November 1935, having completed 217,536 miles.

Representing the tanks, M&SWJR No 14 (*middle*) was thus renumbered from No 4 in 1914 to make way for the 4-4-0 seen above. It is seen, also in M&SWJR red livery, resting between duties on the GWR at Swindon Junction in mid-1923, coupled to a GWR shunter's truck. Renumbered by the GWR as 843 in November 1923 – shedded at Andover Junction at the time – it was withdrawn less than three years later, in August 1926, by then stationed at Swindon Town.

The third photograph shows an example of an ex-M&SWJR loco in GWR guise. Here running as No 1336, the former No 12 makes a delightful picture as it enters Cheltenham Leckhampton station on its final run, hauling a Gloucestershire Railway Society railtour on 9 May 1953. Having taken the train to Andover, then as far as Swindon Junction on the return, 1336 was put back into store (from whence it had emerged after 13 months for this last sortie), the last ex-M&SWJR locomotive to survive. Having been a resident of Reading shed since February 1926, it was finally withdrawn on 27 February 1954 and cut up just over two months later, exactly 60 years after construction. *MJS collection (2)/W Potter, Neville Bridger collection*

Andoversford

As mentioned on page 6, our journey starts at the northern end of the covered route, at Andoversford, 7 miles east of Cheltenham. The true M&SWJR metals began almost immediately after leaving the station, so No 31619, seen entering the platform on 5 March 1960, is still on the ex-GWR route. Although not recorded, the train enjoying the late-winter sunshine is likely to be the early afternoon departure from Cheltenham. Displaying the appropriate BR headcode for a passenger train, No 31619 and its consist will embark on the largely single-line run to Andover – and thence to Southampton – just after this stop. Although the route to Southampton had been opened for passengers in August 1891, with a station on the other side of Andoversford, the GWR refused to allow the M&SWJR trains to stop here until 1 October 1904, leaving travellers a walk of half a mile between the two railways' facilities. At the time of this shot, No 31619 was two-thirds of its way through it stay at Eastleigh shed, later going to Norwood Junction and Guildford, from where it was withdrawn in December 1965. *Gerald Adams*

Crossing to the down platform, we see an unidentified '55XX' 2-6-2T entering the station with a branch-line train from Banbury/Kingham typical of the latter days of services here. Note how the station nameboard still retains the original nomenclature, despite the station having been known as 'Junction' since 1904. The platforms are tidy and weed-free, as is the trackbed; the *de rigueur* fire buckets hang ready; and the goods shed is decorated with holiday posters.

The same view on 17 October 2002 would seem to belie the fact that a railway ever existed here, but the linking proofs are the trees to the left and the tall pine above the station chimneys in the 'past' shot and peering over the rooftops in this view. For many years after closure the site was left moribund but has been developed here as a collection of executive housing, appropriately called Pine Halt. Built in the mid/late-1990s, the two houses on the right occupy a line roughly echoing the old station buildings. *MJS collection/MJS*

Looking back towards Cheltenham, the generous canopies of the main station building (on the left) and the smaller waiting room on the down platform are a feature of this view of No 5514 running into the station with a Banbury train. Although the date is unrecorded, the engine bears an 85B shedplate, placing it between January 1955, when it was transferred to Gloucester (Horton Road) from Swindon, and a withdrawal date of November 1960. A porter waits with a packet in his hand – presumably for this train – while on the near platform what looks to be another photographer watches the arrival. Elsewhere the station is adorned with a selection of posters and a well-tended small garden on the down platform.

Once again, the trees are the giveaway to the location. In this view of 17 October 2002, although they have undoubtedly grown over the ensuing 40 or more years, their line and shape is unmistakeable. The car standing in Pine Halt is very close to the position of the porter in the above view. *David Lawrence, Hugh Davies collection/MJS*

On 10 March 1956 Richard Casserley made a trip along our route with his father. Once more enjoying bright late-winter sunshine, this is his view from the carriage window as the train restarts from Andoversford for Southampton. Judging by the mass of parcels on the platform, the train has just divested itself of a load, leaving the porter with his trolley to tidy up. Between the porter and the end coach, a 15mph warning sign indicates that some trackwork is being/has been under way; and smoke above the waiting room canopy (caught nicely in the carriage window reflection) could indicate the presence of a loco shunting the stock seen in the goods yard.

Once again, the only clue to location is the presence of the pine trees to the right. In this view on 17 October 2002, the Peugeot 205 stands on the line of the platform, roughly adjacent to the telegraph pole in the upper view.
Richard Casserley/MJS

This view is looking out of the opposite side of the carriage, taken this time by Richard's father, but nearly two months after the view on the previous page. On 1 May 1956 the simple but not unattractive station building is seen more clearly, duly adorned with posters advertising both train times and a holiday destination. A sign announces 'You may TELEPHONE from here' in the main platform entrance, while at the far end of the up platform the lower-quadrant signal indicates an imminent arrival.

Again it is the presence of the pines that reveals, despite appearances, that this was once the site of the station. So expertly have the developers obliterated even any semblance of previous outlines, that one wonders if the present inhabitants are aware of the historical importance of their location. *H. C. Casserley/MJS*

In an undated view – probably from the mid-to-late-1950s – the south-easterly aspect shows the bridge over th᳓ A40 road immediately at the end of the platforms, followed by the former GWR route to Kingham and Banbur᳓ to the left and the M&SWJR line to the right. Two lines of mixed wagon types stand between the two route᳓ opposite the junction signal box and the healthy collection of semaphore signals it controls. Elsewhere the wate᳓ column stands ready, as does the brazier used during the winter months, and the platforms look tidy and we᳓ cared for. The sleepers nearest to the camera, however, do look as though they could benefit from a fres᳓ delivery of ballast!

The trees again provide the clue in this October 2002 view. Those seen between the right-hand house and th᳓ lamp standard are taller versions of those seen immediately to the right of the bridge parapet in the 'past' pictur᳓ the others in the earlier view have been swept away in the modern development, opening the vista to those o᳓ the right, which had previously been part of the station entrance. This angle is actually slightly further back alon᳓ the old platform line, to prevent us staring almost blankly into the garden wall! *Neville Bridger collection/MJS*

The photographer has moved to the end of the platform, providing a closer view of the junction on 6 May 1960. The sidings are now emptier and there is the first sign of a run-down in traffic, with grass appearing in the sidings tracks; otherwise, little has changed since the view opposite, apart from the junction signals having been renewed, now boasting metal arms and tubular post. Even the dull weather looks the same!

The erstwhile A40(T) has been relegated to a side road into Andoversford village, following the use of the former trackbed to upgrade the busy trunk road. Thus the road is quiet now, compared to previously, no doubt to the great relief of those living by it! With the railway gone, the bridge has also been removed, leaving this rather uninspiring version of the earlier view. *Neville Bridger collection/MJS*

Opposite Another undated view, but on a happier day as far as the weather is concerned, depicts the junction signal box in all its glory. All lines are obviously still open and the box itself looks in excellent condition, even down to the 'convenience' annex, but the sidings are weed-strewn, with grass now claiming even more of a foothold. The M&SWJR route can just be seen on the extreme right, accessed by the signalman across the long boardwalk, straddling the main view here looking towards Kingham. Opened on 1 August 1891, in time with the official arrival of the M&SWJR route, the box was reduced to ground-frame status on 15 October 1962 with the end of passenger services on the Banbury-Cheltenham line. Final closure came on 23 December 1964.

The far horizon is the only clue today, with the possible exception of the boundary hedge on the far side of the road. The car is close to where the box stood, with the current A40 trunk road now subsuming the previous railway alignment. Here the tarmac engulfs the ex-GWR route, while in the distance, as can be seen, the road curves right to pick up the M&SWJR trackbed for a short distance, thereby forming an effective Andoversford bypass. *Rod Blencowe collection, MJS collection/MJS*

Those overgrown sidings are again seen here, now in the foreground as No 31791, bearing a 71A (Eastleigh) shedplate, prepares to head south away from the station, seen in the background, on 9 September 1961. That this is the very last service passenger train from Cheltenham over the M&SWJR route can be judged by the heads – and bodies where possible! – hanging out of virtually every available opening. This has to be mostly peopled by enthusiasts! The fireman and signalman exchange tokens, allowing the train to proceed. The grin on the face of the former no doubt evidences some comment regarding the nature – and number? – of the passengers! There are many cameras being pointed at the two men – one wonders where those photographs are now. Note the 15mph sign for trains approaching the station area, the approach ground signal and the small iron guard on the boardwalk, preventing the signalman from overstepping his mark. *Neville Bridger collection*

Withington

A peaceful scene at Withington in latter days, looking south. The station signal box is empty, having been close in 1956 as a fully-functioning box, and on 24 November 1957 as a ground frame; the tracks are certainly und attack from Mother Nature in the down loop, and the platforms are beginning to look unkempt, with the statio building on the up platform demolished following reduction to 'Unstaffed Halt' status on 28 May of the same yea The station signboard stands defiant, as does the diminutive waiting shelter, but otherwise the end is in sigh Initially double-track both north to Andoversford and south to Foss Cross, singling took place from 9 July 192 Note how, beyond the bridge, the track falls away steeply on a falling gradient.

The peaceful air is also present today, but with an entirely different aura. Over the four decades since closur not only have the tracks and all structures been removed by October 2002, but also the undergrowth has bee left to its own devices, resulting in this mini-jungle. The outline of the down platform can just be made out as diagonal line from lower left to middle right, but without the distinct line of bricks and edging stones, even th has been 'smoothed'. The only visitors here nowadays are the numerous pheasants grubbing among the tree The overbridge survives, but is totally obscured by the verdant growth. *Neville Bridger collection/MJS*

Right This is the view from the up platform on 24 September 1960, looking north towards Andoversford, 3 miles away. Again, the Dutton & Co signal box is deserted, but in surprisingly fine condition considering that it has been closed for four years. Trains are still running, but the grass encroaching into the view opposite is also evident here. The corrugated iron hut – a lamp store? – also looks as though it has not been use for quite some time. The floor shelter atop the stairs to the box is losing a panel and the 'softening' of the platform surface is more obvious in this view. Note how the access to the siding is only to be had from the down line, with no other obvious crossover point for trains from the south. The sharp right curve in the distance

came about after the realignment of the up track on singling; the down loop rails were extended in 1942 to reach that curve, to cope with heavy wartime traffic. *John Spencer Gilks*

Below The site of Withington station was – and still is – somewhat isolated from its village (population still only 158 at the time of closure!). As the village is not exactly large even today, the prospect for passenger traffic must always have been limited. As can be seen from this view taken on the same day as the one above, the presence of a railway is not obvious and even the signboard appears a mite embarrassed at pointing to the location! The actual entrance was through the gate, with the pathway to the right leading to the previously seen overbridge and beyond. In 2002 this layout is predominantly intact, with only the removal of the sign and the encroachment of modern fencing tidying up the aspect and narrowing the drive. The gate has been replaced by a more modern metal version, with a twin appended to enclose the access to the bridge. *John Spencer Gilks*

Continuing to the overbridge, this was the view down on to the station site on a dull summer's day in 1935. Th[e] previously mentioned crossover to the short goods loop can be seen, together with the sharp convergence int[o] single track for the journey northwards. Apart from the brick-built station building – opened on 16 March 189[?] for goods traffic – facilities are rudimentary as befits a wayside halt somewhat isolated from its source of revenu[e]. All the infrastructure seen here was provided from new and served the station without alteration until the en[d]. The rural aspect is clearly seen stretching to the horizon.

Incredibly this is the same view! Such has been the neglect of the railway infrastructure since closure that th[e] verdant undergrowth has developed unchecked. Now, in 2002, the only inhabitants are birds, predominant[ly] pheasants, which presumably enjoy the peace and seclusion that the trees grant them! Although not discernib[le] from this angle, a rise in the ground left of centre and to the left of the 'crooked' tree to the right marks the outlin[e] of the old platforms. *Neville Bridger collection/MJS*

On the face of it, little has changed in the 25 years since the mid-1930s view opposite. On 5 July 1958 the basic structures survive, the gated entrance to the up platform still stands open and the station nameboard is as before. The fencing behind the latter, however – and indeed, along the whole of the platform – has been changed from wooden boarding to post-and-wire; a telegraph pole has sprouted behind the corrugated iron building, which in turn has lost its hoardings and is now locked shut; trees are growing around the site, the one on the right nearly swallowing the waiting shelter; the platforms now wear a patina of age; and all lighting and signalling has been removed. Meanwhile, grass makes a bid between the rails on the down loop – an indication that services only use the up platform – and what appears to be a short rake of engineer's wagons sit in the loop.

The barrow crossing and neat platform edging have gone, but the mounds of the platforms themselves remain. The sloping ramp of the down side is situated immediately to the right of the twin tree trunks that now grace the old trackbed, and the up platform carves a shadowy diagonal line upwards from the left to the centre of this October 2002 view. Displaying the neglect of the old permanent way site, the ground underfoot here is very uneven! *John Spencer Gilks/MJS*

Above Seen from a Cheltenham-Southampton train on 10 March 1956, there is some semblance of occupation less than three months from closure as a fully functioning station. A seat still graces the platform and there are remains of posters on the hoarding decorating the hut. Elsewhere, telegraph wires droop from the pole to the station building, signals are in place and the far loop 'furniture' is still extant – all had gone by the time of the 'past' view on the previous page. *R. M. Casserley*

Below The date is 19 July 1963 and track-lifting leaves absolutely no doubt that the end has arrived. A permanent way gang surveys the crossover fitting, while No 2872 waits to undertake further shunting before removing recovered trackwork from the site. Bearing in mind that the crossover was the only means of accessing the other track at Withington, it would be interesting to learn precisely how the engine would extricate itself from within the rake of wagons, especially as the loop is blocked with piles of sleepers! Note the signal box stripped bare, the wagon bases waiting their turn in the old bay space behind the up platform (nearest the camera) and the caterpillared 'Vale' crane to the left. *Neville Bridger collection*

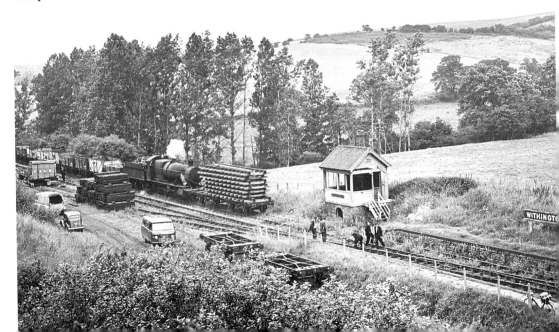

A mile or so south of Withington the railway passed Cassey Compton. As can be seen, the track carved its way through a chalk cutting here, at the approach to Chedworth Woods. On 5 July 1958 the fireman of No 31639 peers up at the photographer as his charge heads south with the 1.52pm Cheltenham St James-Southampton service. Again single track here since 1928, the chalk-loving flora obviously enjoys the relative peace, with only the occasional train to disturb it. Although just another 'U' Class loco at this time, midway through its sojourn at Eastleigh shed, No 31639 was to achieve some sort of notoriety by being the last of the class to be withdrawn – together with No 31791, on 5 June 1966 – and starring on no fewer than seven 'end of steam on the SR' railtours since the beginning of that year. Surely, some sort of record? *John Spencer Gilks*

Chedworth

Above Between Withington and Chedworth stood the 498-yard Chedworth Tunnel, a little over 5 miles from Andoversford. On 20 February 1960, with the remains of winter snows reflecting on the coach side, No 3162? approaches the tunnel, at the southern limit of Chedworth Woods, at the head of the 1.52pm Cheltenham St James-Southampton service. Note the general lie of the land and the angle of the tunnel mouth to the track. Obviously care was needed from the builders to ensure that the bore stayed true to traffic requirement throughout. *John Spencer Gilks*

Above right The other side: later in 1960, in warmer days, an unidentified Class 'U' 2-6-0 sweeps away from the southern portal towards the Chedworth stop with that same 1.52pm Cheltenham St James-Southampton service. This wonderful panoramic shot amply portrays the railway threading its way between the twin escarpments of the tributary of the nearby River Coln, and shows why rails are far less obtrusive to the surrounding countryside than roads. Carving just the width of land needed for the traffic and motive power, the line feels part of the scenery, without the intrusive scars that roads so often inflict on our green and pleasant land. In no way does the train here seem out of place with the obviously settled dwellings and chicken houses in the foreground. *John Spencer Gilks*

Right Swinging through roughly 90 degrees from the view above, that same 'U' – looking under a glass as though it could be No 31795, which was a regular on the line – begins to slow for the Chedworth stop on 24 September 1960. Again, with the engine's smoke mirroring that from a nearby house, and the train's colours – maroon coaches in sympathy with ridge tile and chimney pot colouration – being wholly sympathetic with the surroundings, the railway slips seamlessly into the scheme of things. Certainly, the occasional trains would not unduly disturb the work on the vegetable patch in the foreground. *John Spencer Gilks*

Above One year on from the previous view, on 10 September 1961, the view has hardly changed. The vegetable patch and its greenhouse – here towards the lower right of the picture – are still in full use as No 5306 heads away from Chedworth with a well-packed RCTS Special train. All looks timeless and permanent, but regular through services had ceased the day before and the whole line was officially closed the day after this view. A Pontypool Road engine at the time, No 5306 would move to Newport (Ebbw Junction) within two months. It was finally withdrawn from 87A (Neath) on 20 July 1964. *John Spencer Gilks*

Above right That September day in 1961 was obviously the day to be on the former M&SWJR – albeit for a sad occasion – as, in addition to the RCTS Special seen on the previous page, there was also one operating in the opposite direction. Seen here from the opposite side of the valley, heading southwards, No 7808 *Cookham Manor* glides past the outskirts of Chedworth with another well-supported Special, this time organised by the Stephenson Locomotive Society. During its British Railways life, *Cookham Manor* served many different depots, but was a servant of Banbury on this date. It also spent three spells at Gloucester (Horton Road), from where it was withdrawn on 15 January 1966. Happily, it escaped the 'grim reaper' to find sanctuary in preservation. *John Spencer Gilks*

THE
RAILWAY CORRESPONDENCE AND
TRAVEL SOCIETY

ITINERARY
OF
" THE EAST MIDLANDER "
NOTTINGHAM to SWINDON WORKS
SUNDAY 6th. MAY 1956

Right On page 25 the brick pillar of a road underbridge parapet can be seen just below the front of the first carriage, between the two houses in the centre of the picture. That same pillar is here seen as the left of the three, with that road snaking its way under the railway in a reverse curve, as the RCTS 'East Midlander' railtour of 6 May 1956 approaches Chedworth station. The two ex-Midland 'Simples', Nos 40489 and 40454, make a splendid sight at the head of their six-coach train on this sunny spring day, with the chicken in the bottom left-hand corner seemingly unperturbed by their passage. Footplate crew of both locomotives look out at the photographer, as do many of the travelling passengers. *Hugh Ballantyne*

Above Chedworth station was a simple affair, with the main building on the down platform, closest to the few residences situated in this part of the village. The rudimentary wood and brick building, as seen in this undated view, was little more than a glorified waiting room. With the state of the embankment to the left and the grass encroaching on to the platform, this looks to be towards the end of services on the line. The gas lamp still hangs underneath the station canopy, but with fewer passengers than of yore to shine on. Unlike Withington, when the route was singled in 1928 Chedworth did not retain its up track, the vacant trackbed being obvious in this view, with the empty platform to the right. *Neville Bridger collection*

Below Judging by the station platform and the attire of the lone passenger welcoming the arrival of the train, there has recently been rain on 12 March 1960. No 31795 slows to call at the station at the head of our old friend the 1.52pm Cheltenham St James-Southampton train. Three fire buckets cling tenaciously to the well-stained 'modesty screen' of the Gents, which, with its open aspect, would not give its visitors total relief if the weather were inclement! One wonders what the small window was for to the side of the urinal. The entrance to the station was past the 1930s-provided lean-to milk loading platform. *John Spencer Gilks*

Right This delightful study is undated, but is probably from the very early years of the 20th century. Certainly it is after June 1902, when this station was opened for traffic, replacing a 150-foot single platform arrangement 2 chains to the south. The sole station building of the latter adorns the up platform, again acting as a waiting shelter. What could well be a party of grandmother, mother and daughter – although the latter appears to be carrying a bundle that could be a baby – walk towards the photographer, their focus squarely on him. Their destination, however, is questionable. Had they been waiting for the train that stands in the up platform, they would surely have been on that platform in readiness for its arrival, whereas if they have arrived at Chedworth on that train they would have crossed the line *behind* the photographer! One must presume, therefore, that it is a posed shot. Note the original, appropriately signposted, urinal and the alternate colouring on the canopy of both platforms, and that at the rear of the train, which is signalled to leave, a person seems to be about to clamber on to the platform! *Neville Bridger collection*

Below Moving forward a good half-century, the station – seen from a departing train on 1 May 1956 – appears little altered apart from that infamous toilet! However, the up line has gone – removed in July 1928 – together with the attendant starter signal. The house on the road up from the station is common to both views. Chedworth, opened in 1892, a full year after the line opened, became an unstaffed halt with effect from 1 February 1954, and was finally closed, with the rest of the route, on 11 September 1961. *H. C. Casserley*

Above In this superb pictorial and panoramic view of the station during its heyday, what could well be the Station Master (there were only ever two staff!) watches the photographer, probably conscious that he is standing in the 'four foot'. A train appears to be signalled, but as the Station Master also operated the signal box, it is probably switched out at this moment, with the signals 'off' both ways! Note the smart and tidy appearance: small flower beds adorn the up platform; the trackbed, barrow (and pedestrian) crossing and platforms are immaculate; the fencing looks new; and the boarding of the canopies and signal box roof cladding all clearly show the two-tone paintwork. Note, however, the apparent absence of any location signage! The 1902 15ft by 12ft signal box, containing 14 levers, was another Dutton & Co structure, very similar in style to that erected at Cerney & Ashton Keynes a year or so earlier. *Neville Bridger collection*

Below Again approximately half a century on, 'how the mighty are fallen'! The house and road bridge remain relatively unchanged, as does the station stone boundary wall, and the down waiting shelter still gives potential relief from the elements, but elsewhere the whole ambience is of dereliction. With the up track gone, grass invades the platform and trees stake claim to the embankment; although a station sign is now provided, both the width and surface condition of the down platform are inferior to the earlier view. *Neville Bridger collection*

Above Yes, this is the same view – or, at least, the closest I could come to it! The fence posts in the top left still mark out the field boundary, and the peak of the gable of that 'house on the hill' can just be made out above the right-hand hedge, confirming the location. Elsewhere the trackbed has been raised in height to match the old platform levels and houses built thereon. One wonders whether the new owners are aware of the heritage beneath their feet... *MJS*

Below A final look at Chedworth, and one that surprises with an unusual example of motive power on the route. On 5 June 1958 ex-WD 'Austerity' No 90685 makes a test trip from Swindon Works. The fireman takes a breather as the engine approaches the station, leaning on the cabside and looking ahead at the photographer. The loco does look clean, but not in the usual ex-Works condition, so it is puzzling as to the nature of the test. A Western Region engine for the first dozen years of its British Railways career, it was a Gloucester (Horton Road) locomotive at the date of this photograph, but transfer was around the corner, as it travelled to Cardiff Canton four months later. A move to the Eastern Region beckoned on 8 December 1962, with withdrawal following on 28 November 1964. *Edwin Wilmshurst*

Foss Cross

Above While Withington was separated from its community, Foss Cross was positively divorced from surrounding habitation! As can be seen from this view, the station was literally in the middle of nowhere, wit the woods and hillsides around Chedworth now replaced by flat, open Gloucestershire countryside. The nam was borrowed from the nearby crossroads on the ancient Roman 'Foss (sic) Way'. The 'East Midlander' railtou of 6 May 1956, seen earlier on page 27, here sweeps into the northern approaches to the station, from the summi of the line, with single track opening out to double. Note the small ground signal and the unusual catch point arrangement, immediately to the right of the third coach. Heads poke from the leading coaches – all apparentl looking backwards towards the photographer – and one passenger looks to be about to drop a duffle bag on t the track! *John Edgington*

Left The other Special alread seen, on page 26, pauses for a sto at Foss Cross, under leaden skies on 10 September 1961, and some o the RCTS tour's participants tak advantage of the opportunity t stretch their legs and visit th isolated location, 583 feet abov sea level, while No 5306's firema rakes coal forward in the tende The creditably clean Pontypoo Road locomotive simmers quietl at the head of its eight-coach trai while all this goes on, somewha unusually – and inappropriately? adorned with an 'Expres Passenger' headcode. Note th relaxed air and sober dress of th tour members, and the relativ absence of cameras, compared t what the scene would be in the 21s century. *Alan Lillywhite, Joh Spencer Gilks collection*

Above Another view of the station from the north. Although undated, this shot is obviously later than that opposite, as the lamp gracing the station signboard has now disappeared. Elsewhere, the track is still in good condition; a couple of goods vehicles have moved on to the siding on the left; the 13ft by 11ft signal box still has its nameboard and 22 levers; the cattle pen still stands at the far end of the up platform; and with seats still extant the platforms do not yet show signs of neglect, so all would seem to indicate a period around 1960. *MJS collection*

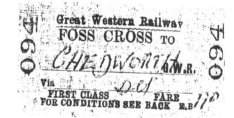

Right Seen from a southbound train on 1 May 1956, the signal box is here in full use, complete with a milk churn, postbox (or is it a covered tap?) and a myriad of telegraph wires arriving at the station. Again, the open countryside can be seen to the left: the remoteness begs the question as to why the station was sited here, 6 miles from Cirencester and only a mile from Chedworth. Situated midway between Cirencester and Withington, it was possibly a useful passing place, but, probably more to the point, there was land available for sidings (which there was not at Chedworth) and there was quarrying nearby. The distinctive soft yellowish local stone was liberally used as ballast on the route. Perhaps incredibly, the location had an engine shed when opened! *H. C. Casserley*

As seen at Withington earlier, 1963 saw the physical end of the line, with track-lifting and the rescue of re-usable items. While that station was seen in July, the scene here at Foss Cross is on a somewhat inclement 28 June. In obviously driving rain, No 6344, with steam clinging to the sodden boiler barrel, pulls forward into the station platform in readiness to shunt the brake-van into position. There is no sign of the crew, but perhaps the guard is watching the fireman in the act of coupling the van to the loco's tender. The rain adds to the general feel of dereliction, with the station noticeboard – itself covering a previous doorway – bereft of information, a motor tyre abandoned on the nearside platform and grass well and truly taking a hold. Compare this with the views of the station on the previous page, only a handful of years earlier.

Given the weather, the tarpaulin over the cab aperture is obviously welcome, although in this view the rain appears to have stopped. The loco has not moved, however, and this is the view looking north, with sleepers at the far end of the platform and the signal box now without its nameboard and with its windows smashed.

Time has now passed and No 6344 has collected some of the 16-ton wagons seen in the background of the first view. The gangers have obviously been at work on the right, with the sidings cut off, and sleepers and chairs summarily dumped, but the ground signal appearing to give access to the running lines! Having wreaked its destruction, No 6344 will return to its home at Gloucester (Horton Road), but not to a great deal more work, as it was withdrawn five months later, on 30 November. *All Neville Bridge collection*

Above Reverting to happier times, and crossing to the up platform, we see No 31808 with the appropriate 'Branch Passenger' headlamp, pausing with its three-coach southbound train on 30 July 1960. A quartet of locals discusses some matter while presumably waiting for a northbound service to arrive. Although all the facilities are obviously in use, including an optimistic parcels barrow, it is disappointing to see the already slightly neglected state of the platform. As can be seen from No 31808's shedplate, the Cheltenham-Southampton trains were the province of SR motive power from Eastleigh, although the coaching stock, including what looks like a Hawksworth design in the centre, is WR. The '4P/3F' 'U' was at Eastleigh for seven months in 1952, then between March 1959 and withdrawal on 27 January 1964. Just visible through the cab spectacle, the fireman watches the photographer take his shot. *Mike Esau*

Right At the start of the 21st century it is virtually impossible – and certainly meaningless in the context of this book – to replicate the above view. This is as close as I could get in 2002, with the still extant station building being the only evidence of the old facilities. As can be seen, the platform area is now totally subsumed beneath a 'jungle', although the actual structure still remains. *MJS*

Once more back on the down platform, this is the view of the station, looking north, on 5 June 1958. Although once again evidencing the remoteness of the situation, the station still represents so many other such facilities throughout the country and a vivid example of why so many perished in the face of road competition. At this date the station noticeboard has its advertising posters, the signal box its own facilities, and the down sidings, to the right, both contain rakes of goods vehicles, showing that there were at least healthy freight needs at the location. With the absence of protecting canopies, passengers standing on the platforms were subject to the sometimes vicious winds that could sweep across this unprotected stretch of Gloucestershire.

To include any sight of the station building, it was necessary on 17 October 2002 to stand in the 'four-foot' but much closer than the above shot, otherwise the view would have totally obliterated by verdant growth. The building can just be glimpsed through the trees, now without chimneys, and the platform also remains as the dark area centre left – what the rubbish bin is doing in this isolated spot is open to conjecture! *Edwin Wilmshurst, Neville Bridger collection/MJS*

Moving slightly further south, the broader station aspect is seen in this undated view, although probably taken during 1960 (see overleaf). No 31803 is seen receiving the 'right away' from the guard to continue its journey southwards with another Cheltenham St James-Southampton train. To the right of the lower-quadrant signal, two box vans stand on the down loop, close to the goods shed and its attendant loading gauge; the latter was replaced by a free-standing version before the end in 1961. From 1902 the trackwork, which here looks to have seen some recent re-ballasting, would have been double both north and south of Foss Cross, but as with other locations it was singled in 1928.

Even at this wider angle it is still unrecognisable as the same place. On the tree line, in the centre of the view, beehives now occupy the trackbed, with the old down platform having totally disappeared. To the left stands an old corrugated hut, quite possibly the one seen in the earlier view, situated on that old down platform. *MJS collection/MJS*

Our final views of Foss Cross show No 31808, previously seen on page 35, now leaving on its southwards journey to Southampton on 30 July 1960. With the fresh ballast and the box van on the down loop, this is almost certainly within a day or two of the picture on the previous page, if not the actual day with another train, but barely a year before closure. Having secured the road ahead, the driver stares at the ground, apparently deep in thought before the next call on his attention. Although showing the grime from its efforts, No 31808 still has signs of its attractive lining on the tender and the small splashers characteristic of the class.

Yes, I know it is hard to believe, but this is the same place! The car, now on the only means of access to the site, is standing roughly where the pointwork was in 1960, immediately to the right of the semaphore signal. As seen before, the growth of vegetation over the almost 40 years since closure is such that, superficially, all trace of the railway has gone and, certainly, to the south of this point, that is literally the case where some industrial units have been built. *Mike Esau/MJS*

Cirencester

Fourteen miles from the beginning of our journey, the railway entered Cirencester from the north-east, crossing the A419 (built on the alignment of the ancient SE-NW Roman Road) just before the station, in the Watermoor area of the town; hence, in 1924, the station attracted this suffix to identify it from the Town station on the GWR's branch from Kemble, which approached from the opposite direction. On 10 September 1961 the RCTS Special seen previously at Chedworth and Foss Cross pauses at Watermoor station for a last passenger train visitation to the site, with bodies everywhere! With the railway closing the following day, presumably these were not all from the train – the presence of young children gazing intently at the loco's cab and the onlookers on the platform seem to indicate local Cirencestrians – but if they were, the tour is going to be delayed! Note the water column on the right, next to the long-lifted up track and no use here to No 5306. Note also the bow-tie (left) and the Scout (right), and the almost total absence of cameras. How times have changed! *Alan Lillywhite, John Spencer Gilks collection*

London and South Western Ry.
787
From WATERLOO
TO
CIRENCESTER
Via ANDOVER JUNCTION.

Looking south on 1 May 1956, a Cheltenham St James-Southampton train receives attention from the station staff unloading parcels and trunks, while what appears to be a '63XX' 'Mogul' approaches from the south. Notice how like so many other situations on the line, the down platform only has a rudimentary waiting shelter, with the main building being on the up side. The water column, seen on the last page, which replaced an earlier L&SWR-style facility in 1919, is here still in use, with the signal box at the far end of the platform and, beyond that, the outline of the local gas works, opened in 1833 and closed in 1939.

Once again, even though it has been said before, this really is the same view! Although a little difficult to see against the bright sunlight, the end-on chimney seen to the left of the station lamp in the earlier view can just be seen through the bush on the left of this shot. The site of the station is now buried beneath the A419 ring road to Stroud, and one wonders how many of the thousands of motorists that use the road annually realise just where they are. The site was also confirmed, while I was taking the photograph, by a local lady, who greatly mourned the passing of the railway, especially with the increasing congestion on local roads to the north and south.
H. C. Casserley/MJS

In the first view, undated but probably during the summer of 1961, we are now midway along the platform, still looking south. The up track has been lifted, following the striking of Bridge 154 – over the original Cricklade-Cirencester road – in early 1960 by a mechanical digger, which rendered the west side of the alignment unsafe. As seen here, a little unusually, the sleepers have been left loosely in situ, with rail dumped at the side, and grass is already growing between some of them. The 19-lever signal box closed with the abandonment of the up line, was subsequently gutted by fire in late 1961 and demolished. Notices, a gas lamp and a seat still remain, however,

on the redundant platform, which no longer gives shelter from the rainy conditions seen here to waiting passengers! In the distance, the previously mentioned gas works building can be seen more clearly, with goods wagons parked alongside, while to the left of the view note how the station boundary, from the adjacent housing, is here delineated by stone blocks, rather than the post and wire of the northern end of the platform.

The date of the second view is 18 July 1964, and the scene is one of total abandonment, final freight services having ceased from 1 April. Not only has nature continued its onslaught on the up line, with rosebay willow-herb in profusion on the trackbed, but the down side is now also under strong attack. By now, the afore-mentioned signal box, seat and gas lamp have all gone, as has the station signboard and gas works chimney top. By this time, although the up track still lies abandoned on the ballast, the sleepers have been removed.

There is absolutely nothing here to positively identify the location, but this was the site in 2002, with the ring road seen approaching one of the many roundabouts on its tour of the town. Sadly, none of the infrastructure visible in the above photographs now remains. *Neville Bridger collection/J. M. Tolson, F. Hornby collection/MJS*

The main station structure at Cirencester was a solid but elegant stone affair, sat squarely midway along the platform on the west (up) side of the line. It was built for the opening of the line from Swindon on 1 November 1883 and remained a terminus until the extension to Andoversford in 1891. In this undated view, seen from the road approach, with a train in the up platform, both tracks are obviously still in use, although perhaps the 'Public Notice' by the gated entrance to the platform is warning of the withdrawal of that nearest the camera. Judging by the presence of raincoats and by the obvious hurry of the workman, with a bag over his shoulder and bike clips already around his ankles, it either is or has been raining and is threatening more. Interesting to see the ten bicycles leaning against the building, unattended, complete with pumps and saddlebags and absolutely no locks or anti-theft devices. Oh, happy days! The adjacent posters advertise the glories of the Gower Coast, Holyhead and some form of labelling! Note the awning for the main entrance to the building.

The second photograph, clearly taken on the same day, shows the other end of the building, showing the Gents toilet block and the presence of one or two cars parked on the approach road. *Both Neville Bridger collection*

As seen on page 41, the up track was lifted at some time around 1960/61 and the rather unusual positioning of sleepers is again in view here, as an unidentified 'U' Class 2-6-0 enters the station with a Southampton train. Once more the photograph is undated, but is probably early 1961, judging by the station furniture on both platforms and the presence of the porter ready for his next duty. Note the previously mentioned concrete blocks acting as the boundary with the adjacent private gardens. The down-side waiting shelter, although of corrugated iron, looks to be clean, airy and welcoming. It was still standing late into the decade, long after any passengers had made use of it.

Again, it is difficult, with cars coursing along the A419, to appreciate that this is the same location in 2002, but the young trees on the right in the earlier view have grown to maturity and now dominate the scene. Incredibly, despite the rest of the site being totally redeveloped and landscaped, obliterating any evidence of a railway ever having been here, those concrete blocks remain, lurking under the leafy canopy and enjoying anonymity. *MJS collection/MJS*

Above Stepping across to the down platform, we are in much happier times, on 6 September 1952. No 6381 slows as it approaches the end of the platform at the head of the 10.10am Cheltenham St James-Southampton train. The late summer morning is warm and sunny, as the impending passengers wait patiently and relaxed for the train to stop. Elsewhere, the station is a fine example of a neat and tidy, well cared for facility, with swept and weedless platform surfaces, posters all in place and undamaged, and parcel trolleys at the ready. A long-term resident of Gloucester (Horton Road) shed, No 6381 transferred allegiance to Pontypool Road on 21 May 1955, from where it was withdrawn on 30 November 1963. *H. C. Casserley*

Below Seven and a half years later, on 20 February 1960, this time the train is bound for Andover Junction behind ex-SR 'Mogul' No 31629. While the station still displays evidence of care and attention and has all the hallmarks of regular operations, the red flag in the up 'four-foot' gives notice of the damage problems to the road bridge immediately to the north of the station. Considered sufficiently unsafe to prevent traffic using the up line this led to the track-lifting already seen; the 'knock-on effect' was that both northbound and southbound services had to use the one set of rails, extending the single-line 'block' working. Note the white-painted building, which had originally been the Station Master's 'house' and was later used by the Locomotive Superintendent and Civil Engineer based at the nearby Works. *Edwin Wilmshurst, Neville Bridger collection*

The next four views are from the southern end of the station, showing changes over time. The first, dated 7 August 1950, two years after Nationalisation, shows a creditably clean 'Manor', No 7818 *Granville Manor*, drawing away from Watermoor station with the 10.05am Cheltenham-Southampton turn, with everything in the picture 'looking the part' – the gangers' hut on the left, the barrow crossing light, signal box and water tower, telegraph wires, signal and point rodding, water column by the loco, the ex-GWR token pick-up post on the right, even down to the 'manicured' trackbed and cess. The warm summer sunshine completes the attractive aspect and, in turn, appears to be making the two railmen working the barrow on the up track less active than perhaps is good for them!

The date of the second view is 10 March 1956, and nothing has changed. At places like this during the 1950s it was undoubtedly the *permanent* way, without the dark clouds of change that would sweep the railway landscape within a decade. The signal box, closed officially on 21 August 1960, has been repainted since the 1950 view, and beyond the substantial, brick-built 15,000-gallon water tank towers over the old Station Master's house. *John Edgington/R. M. Casserley*

Another four years on, and things have most definitely taken a turn for the worse. In a summer scene from 1960, services are still running, evidenced by the presence of the signalman, but, as previously seen, now only on the down line. Notice how the marks of the sleepers undulate the ballast, while some of the rails have been dumped. Perhaps the later placing of sleepers throughout the platform area was to discourage trespass. The small fence and lamp by the barrow crossing – seen to the left of No 7818 on page 45 – have also been dispensed with. This crossing was installed not only for the use of passengers to access the down platform, but also, in the immediate pre-First World War period, for the transportation across the permanent way of milk churns, recognising the importance of this traffic at the time. Such was the volume of this traffic in the early 1920s that a milk van was stabled on a siding behind the 19-lever signal box and picked up by the evening down passenger train. An addition, however, from the above views, is the appearance of what looks to be an attempt at a small station garden at the side of the signal box. Presumably a noble effort by a member of staff, it now seems to be 'going to seed', as does the rest of the platform, with grass beginning to gain a foothold.

With the elimination of the railway, the bridge over Gas Lane was removed, leaving the aspect much changed. This is the view from the other side of the bridge to the erstwhile station site in 2002, showing how successful the industrial unit and its landscaping have been in covering the railway's tracks! The trees to the right have enjoyed the passage of time and only the presence of some remaining trackbed embankment behind me as I took this photograph reinforced the location. *MJS collection/MJS*

Already seen at Chedworth and Foss Cross, the RCTS's 'East Midlander' railtour of 6 May 1956 has now reached Cirencester, again pausing for the participants to stretch their legs and explore the station site. Judging by the fireman glimpsed on top of the tender of train engine No 40454, the loco is taking water, with, presumably, No 40489's own thirst having been slaked. The fireman of the latter watches his driver make his way back to the front, after exchanging words with a very important-looking gentleman in raincoat and trilby. To the right, the pipe-toting enthusiast in his waistcoat, his jacket abandoned, seems to indicate that the day is warming up. A handful of onlookers are on the platform, while to the left a young spotter looks on, his box Brownie over his shoulder. Between him and the train stands a token post, bearing a warning that speed should not exceed 15mph when using it.

Again appearances are deceptive in this October 2002 view, looking across the road from the remaining piece of embankment to the entrance of AE's industrial site, but the houses, to the right in the above view, still exist, albeit now hidden behind the greatly enhanced tree line. *John Edgington/MJS*

These three views show the Works complex adjacent to the south-west boundary of the station. The main route's curvature through the station is well exemplified in the first view, looking north on 10 March 1956. The station is to the right, while the Works is on the extreme left, with a goods shed between and Cirencester's church spire just discernible to the right of the main Works building. Rail access to the latter was courtesy of a curving siding which skirted the abutments of the Gas Lane underbridge. A fan of sidings then served Works, goods shed, carriage and wagon works and a building for running repairs.

Cirencester Works, opening in 1895, brought real importance to this part of the M&SWJR. Selected as there was insufficient space at Swindon for the necessary infrastructure, Cirencester thereafter became the railway's

headquarters for operational purposes, with important individuals from General Manager Sam Fay downwards based there. Economically, too, it was important to have maintenance and repair facilities 'in house', to avoid sending locomotives to Nine Elms in London and coaching and wagon stock to Gloucester. The main building seen in the second view, also taken on 10 March 1956, is the 1903 extension of the loco shop, with the 1915-dated machine shop to the left. In front, latter-day 'Steptoe & Son' rag-and-bone men prepare to sift through the detritus and load their wagon, while their horse stands patiently. Elsewhere an old van stands by the abandoned loading gauge and all manner of tyres and rubbish are piled between the tracks.

Viewed from another angle less than two months later, on 1 May 1956, there have been some changes, not least additions to the pile of discards! Wire and bent metal is interspersed with dumped cars, which, by the look of them, not even the most avid vintage car collector would want! Meanwhile two horseboxes are ready for use, standing on the spur to the original carriage and wagon repair shops. The Works closed on 26 October 1925 and the doors are here fully shut, but to little purpose, as the roof is missing! Note the '1915' plaque on the brickwork of the machine shop. *R. M. Casserley (2), H. C. Casserley*

South Cerney

Above Looking south through South Cerney station, 3 miles from Cirencester, on 24 April 1958, it looks to be in reasonable condition and ready for business, although isolated from its community by half a mile. The signalman's bicycle leans against the 14ft by 12ft 14-lever signal box, while on the other platform a seat awaits the next waiting passenger, and the plain but serviceable station building does likewise. Both platforms were 258 feet in length, with the adjacent horse dock of 67 feet. The way south is seen through the many-arched bridge that spans the tracks, providing the eastern exit from the village towards Cerney Wick. *R. M. Casserley*

Below Moments later 'Standard' 4-6-0 No 76065, bearing a 'through freight' lamp code, ambles through the station with a very mixed goods train bound for the Southern Region, containing, among other things, wood and oil. Note the station sidings on the left with a rake of wooden-bodied 12-ton wagons, out of sight in the above view, and the abandoned 'billy-can' prominent on the platform! In the inter-war years the goods yard saw much coal and timber traffic, as well as gravel extracted locally and moved to the railway for transhipment and onward transportation. An unusual visitor to the line, No 76065 went new to Eastleigh on 27 August 1956 and spent the whole of its life at that shed, expiring on 31 October 1965. *R. M. Casserley*

Superficially little has changed since No 76065 trundled through with its varied cargo, but in this undated view the station has certainly been left to nature and grass has begun to sprout in abundance on the edges of the platforms. Probably around 1961, both signal box and station still have their signs, and a starter semaphore remains to control the road in the left distance, but on this platform the posters have been summarily torn from their boards and the station building now wears a very unkempt air. This signal box was a 1942 GWR replacement for the more squat and much more attractive (1900) original that sat at the foot of the platform slope, 100 feet or so to the north. The opening beneath the platform to accommodate the point rodding and signal wires can be readily seen in front of the 'new' box. Closing on 11 September 1961, with the ending of passenger services, it remained in use as a ground frame until 1 July 1963, when goods traffic was withdrawn.

When built in 1883, the station sat amidst open countryside, but before long gravel extraction began to seriously affect the area, creating a lake behind the box by the early years of the 20th century. Since the departure of the railway, the area to the east and south-east of the station has been further developed by gravel extraction, leading to the creation of a myriad of lakes and a generally watery environment. This is the view from a footpath that was the sole remaining access point to the site in October 2002. To the left, behind the fencing, lies a housing development, while through the barbed wire the trackbed has been affected by the extraction, falling away over the site of the down platform towards the water. *Neville Bridger collection/ MJS*

Orientation for the 'present' view opposite was by means of the bridge arch adjacent to the station building in this view, with the current footpath using the inner edge of the platform as its line. Another undated photograph, but thought to be around 1962, shows the slight camber on the track as it sweeps through the station, followed by a reverse curve in the distance on its way to Cricklade. Initially the simple brick building and its platform were the only facilities provided, but this was changed around 1900 when the second platform, with its wood and corrugated iron shelter, was installed, together with a crossing loop and the original signal box. For many years there was a starter signal on the down platform, with a white patch painted on the bridge parapet to ease sighting by the loco crews. In this view that patch has disappeared and the wider of the bridge supports now shows only plain brickwork. The chimneys of the main building were originally built much taller, but suffering, perhaps, from stress or poor construction, they were rebuilt at this lower level in February 1910.

Turning round from the 'present' view opposite, we now look towards the bridge and its arches, which are still there but now totally camouflaged by the verdant growth. The garden fencing to the right roughly mirrors the line of the station building above. Today the trackbed is totally inaccessible here, apart from the small area immediately below the bridge arches. *Neville Bridger collection/MJS*

In much happier days, in 1935, the station has a much more businesslike appearance. On the up platform (left) station flowerbeds are giving colour and appeal to the waiting area, with parcels barrow and trolley ready for the movement of any items; gas lamps stand strategically stationed to give light to travellers, posters abound, and a 'You may TELEPHONE from here' no doubt provides a facility little present elsewhere in the village at this time. The wooden fencing, crossing light, loading gauge and semaphore signals at the far end all add to the sum of necessary infrastructure. Elsewhere, on the down side, there is another token post, the signal box is the original squat structure, replaced in 1942, and the small waiting shelter has its side window partly smothered by a magnificent tree, which again is absent in later views.

As previously stated, access to the trackbed through the station is now nigh on impossible and, indeed, it is fenced off from the area underneath the arches. Peering over this fencing, however, replicating the above vantage point graphically shows the problems of anyone wishing to walk the line! *Neville Bridger collection/MJS*

The approach to South Cerney station curved into the adjacent yard from the west, at the start of the rise in the road for the overbridge. On 24 April 1958 the photographer's pre-war Hillman Minx, complete with Plymouth registration and original-style 'AA' badge, stands in glorious isolation at the far end of the 'drive'. Access to the platform was at this time an open gap between the rudimentary post-and-wire fence that had replaced the earlier wooden one, and the main station building was around the corner of that structure, here on the right. Beyond is the signal box, with the incumbent's bike still parked alongside.

By October 2002 the growth of the surrounding trees shades the view of the houses that have been built on the site. Incorporating the siding space that was to the left of Henry Casserley's view, the small estate of dwellings has totally obliterated any possibility of recognising this as being the way in to the old station. *H. C. Casserley/MJS*

M. & S.W.R. Station, South Cerney.

A final look back at South Cerney around 1910: the station very much looks the part, even substantial, with its alternately coloured brickwork, climbing plants and small platform gardens, Midland Railway poster boards and Gentlemen's facility at this end. Somewhat surprisingly, however, there are no seats or awning for waiting passengers outside the building – the former are further along the platform! A station official peers suspiciously at the photographer, close by the ladder and loaded trolley by the gas lamp, while at this end of the platform what appear to be two beer barrels await attention. The station sign is not confused, as the location was originally named 'Cerney & Ashton Keynes' by the railway, the name being shortened to 'Cerney' shortly after this photograph, and to that of the nearby village in July 1924. Note the presence of the original signal box – the paint on its lower windows wearing off – and the siting of the up semaphore signal on the down side of the track, to aid sighting by the engine crews. Note also the clock on the station wall, in the position later taken up by the previously seen 'Telephone' sign.

More *The Day of the Triffids* than *The Railway Children*, this is view that greets an inquisitive onlooker in 2002, with tentacles of ivy attempting to reach out to the unwary! As can be seen, the 'opening' of the area to nature and the inherent water table has encouraged the growth in arboriculture. Only the bridge parapet, in the bottom left-hand corner, gives the game away. *Neville Bridger collection/MJS*

Cricklade

From South Cerney the railway ran in virtually a straight line south-east for nearly 3½ miles to Cricklade, where once more we see the RCTS railtour of 10 September 1961, making its steady way northwards behind No 5306, this time pausing at Cricklade station. We are now in Wiltshire, the boundary with Gloucestershire being roughly halfway from South Cerney. Again the passengers have been given the opportunity to explore the station area and stream away from their seats to inspect what takes their fancy. Several, possibly including the two ladies climbing the platform slope, are intent on investigating the signal box, no doubt to the amusement/bemusement of the signalman! The 12ft by 11ft 6in box was graced with 14 levers – eight controlling signals and the remainder controlling points, with no spares. Token-catchers again stand on either side of the tracks, complete with protective netting, with a pile of sleepers on the left providing a somewhat precarious platform for handling or retrieving. Elsewhere, to the left of the platform a Wickham trolley stands in the nearby siding, with oil tanks this end and parcels and goods vans at the far end of the station. A total of four sidings was provided, serving horse dock, cattle pens, milk platform and a goods shed. One or two cameras are evident, but otherwise conspicuous by their absence. *Alan Lillywhite, John Spencer Gilks collection*

In another view of the station from the north, at around the same period as the previous one, what appear to be coal wagons stand in the sidings behind the box, while more parcels and goods vans (one smothered in tarpaulin) wait their next turn of duty at the far end of the platform. As with most of the stations on this line, the main building stood on the side closest to the named locality, with only a small rudimentary shelter on the other platform. This initially stood closer to the platform edge, before the area was widened early in 1919. An attractive veranda was added to the southern aspect of the signal box around 1944. With 'healthy' grass growth on the platform edge, the station has seen some happier times.

After the closure of the railway the trackbed was utilised by the highways authority to provide a link road to the B4040 to Malmesbury, with the space on either side used for new housing. In mid-afternoon sun in October 2002, the cyclist and motorists are probably blissfully unaware of the significance of the roadway! The row of garages in Saxon Close on the left, reflecting the fact that Cricklade boasts itself as an ancient Saxon town, are roughly in line with the old sidings. *Neville Bridger collection/MJS*

Above Another view of the signal box on 10 September 1961, this time after the throng have sated their appetite for inspection of the box and station buildings. The guard, standing on the down platform with flags in hand, waits patiently for the photographers to grab their last shots of No 5306, whose tender is glimpsed to the right, obviously keen to have the train restart its journey. Although officially closing to passenger traffic the following day, goods survived until 1 July 1963. *Rod Blencowe, Neville Bridger collection*

Below Modern trains are extremely limited for space and have problems admitting wheelchairs or even bikes. One wonders how would they fare with this! In an undated view, but probably around the late 1950s, a porter struggles valiantly with a canoe, desperately trying to find a way of fitting it into the van of the leading coach of this northbound train! The pained expression on his face seems to indicate that the photographer would be better served giving him a hand! Meanwhile, the driver of No 31791 watches the exercise patiently – and sympathetically? *Hugh Davies*

In an undated view estimated to be around 1948, a northbound freight trundles through Cricklade, seen from the 312-foot down platform. The signalman prepares to mount the steps to his box, having exchanged the single-line tokens with the driver of the train, but waits for a station colleague, who approaches with overcoat slung casually over his shoulder. Milk churns and the once ubiquitous parcels trolley adorn the platforms, while posters liberally decorate both sets of buildings. Milk was once a very important commodity for this station, with a 175-foot loading platform especially provided. Note the platform gas lamps and the two under the station canopy – these were all changed on a number of occasions, with the original gas type replaced in 1910, 1913 and 1917!

The success in landscaping the area, since the house building began, to totally disguise the original use of the land is readily apparent in this northwards view of the above scene, in October 2002. No doubt the road builders were very grateful of the hard work already done by railway navvies in carving out a near flat surface, leading to much reduced effort for them in creating this new road. *Neville Bridger collection/MJS*

Another undated view, but around the 1961 period, shows the tarpaulined goods vehicle in the 85-foot end-loading horse-dock bay. There have been few changes since 1948, the most notable being the absence of the twin gas lamps underneath the main station building awning. Otherwise the station sleeps between the few daily trains, much as it has done for years. Note how, in concert with all the other stations on our route – with the exception of Swindon Town – passengers were faced with crossing the tracks on the simple, often slippery, wooden barrow crossing at the platform ends. No Health & Safety Executive in those days!

On the face of it, what we see today is a totally unexceptional piece of roadway. Perhaps only an eagle-eyed rail enthusiast would identify that the topography of the route looks suspiciously good for 'just a road'. On the right, in 2002, Parsonage Farm Close leads towards the old bay and the goods yard beyond. *Neville Bridger collection/MJS*

Once again we encounter our old friend the RCTS 'East Midlander' railtour of 6 May 1956, which has reached Cricklade on its southwards journey to Swindon, having originated at Nottingham. The two ex-Midland 'Simples' blow off as they prepare to restart, their road cleared by the semaphore. In the bright afternoon sunshine the two look truly magnificent. On the left, what looks to be an ex-GWR 0-6-0PT waits for the road at the head of a mixed freight, presumably 'wrong road' to allow the passage of the special, which is about to cross a culvert bridge. To the right, wooden 12-ton and steel 16-ton open wagons stand with a box van in the goods shed siding. At this time No 40489 was a Gloucester (Barnwood) resident – being withdrawn from there on 13 August 1960 – while companion No 40454 was visiting from Nottingham, from where it ended its days on 8 October 1960. *Hugh Ballantyne*

Viewed from a carriage, looking south, a Cheltenham-Southampton train restarts its journey in April 1959. The transition from double to single track is evident immediately before the lone semaphore in the distance. The parapets of the bridge over the culvert seen opposite can just be made out as the tracks begin to come together. Beyond that, the up distant stands by the parapets of the B4041 Cricklade-Wootton Bassett road. The locomotive is unknown, but interesting: it is a tender engine but does not appear to be an ex-GWR example – the cylinder sides are vertical and it would certainly not be a 'Castle' or 'King' – and although it could be an ex-SR 'N' by the cab spectacle, there does not appear to be evidence of smoke deflectors.

Technically I should have been standing on the white line in the middle of the road, but I did want to continue taking photographs on this day in October 2002! The B road mentioned above is now a much-enlarged affair and is signified in this view by the announcement of the roundabout ahead, pointing in the direction of West Swindon to the right. Beyond that road junction the trackbed survives, but probably little known and less cared about by the local residents. *Mike Esau/MJS*

Once more looking back towards Cirencester, here are three comparative views. In the first, taken on 15 March 1958, the photographer's father's car stands in glorious isolation at the side of the bay tracks, seemingly the only vehicle wishing to use the station approach road. Beyond the pile of coal on the extreme right are more box vans, this time parked behind the station building, rather than in the bay platform as seen before. In the distance, the tracks, already curving through the platforms, sharpen the angle to pass under the original Cricklade-Malmesbury road overbridge not captured in the photographs on earlier pages. By the look of the concrete posts lying casually dumped on the left, the boundary post to the approach road could be in danger of imminent replacement.

While the above view could indicate a lack of traffic, the appearance of No 7808 *Cookham Manor* just a few minutes later, together with the clutch of waiting passengers under the platform canopy, dispels the illusion. The signalman, at the far end of the platform, watches proceedings as the travellers wait for the train to stop. Note the seat by the nameboard on the left, slightly unusually positioned at the extreme end of the platform by the ramp to the barrow crossing.

Incredibly, such has been the total masking of the station site by subsequent development, the entrance to Pittsfield, where the Peugeot 305 estate stands, is roughly comparable with the seat and signage in the earlier views, and although one solitary tree poked its head above the up platform in those shots, one presumes that today's stand of trees is a later planting. Note again how easy the railway had made it for the road engineers. *R. M. Casserley (2)/MJS*

Our final view at Cricklade, on 15 March 1958, revisits the aspect looking south as the route leaves the station area and approaches the inter-station single-track layout. The left foreground track is from the bay and up sidings, joining the main line immediately by that culvert bridge. The wooden-post semaphores stand guard over the entrance to and exit from the station, with the down starter, closest to the camera, reputedly being the very last original ex-M&SWJR signal in use on the line. Note its balance-weight and arm mounted high up the post.

The curve of the track is today camouflaged by the design of the road layout approaching and utilising the roundabout, but, again, beyond the latter the trackbed remains. *H. C. Casserley/MJS*

Blunsdon

Compared to most of the stations on the stretch of the old M&SWJR that we are featuring in this volume, that at Blunsdon was more a ramshackle halt than anything else! On a sunny early summer's day in 1935, the edifice awaits the next train, with what looks to be a porter standing guard on the platform. Surely his could not have been a particularly arduous job, although at one time 60 17-gallon milk churns a day would be handled here! The white gate gave access to the 176-foot split-level platform, seen here just beyond the small hut that housed a ground frame; interestingly it has wire mesh over the window, and boasted just two levers, to control the only siding on site. It is interesting to note the difference in levels of the wooden platform between that in front of the corrugated iron pagoda-style 'station building' and the station nameboard, just visible beyond. The wooden structure alongside the main building seems to serve no purpose, but perhaps once had a canopy to protect the milk from the effects of the elements. A gangers' hut stands on the opposite side of the track.

In contrast, the present-day preservation operation, based here, has made Blunsdon a much more important venue. The original site was where the small hut and grounded coach are now, in the centre of the picture beyond the fencing, whereas the present platform is further to the north, as can be seen. Since taking over the site, the restorers have created a double-track layout. *Neville Bridger collection/MJS*

A slightly wider view from the road overbridge on 8 June 1934 gives a tantalising glimpse of the short siding running off to the left immediately after the bridge; at 180 feet it was capable of holding nine wagons. Notice that it is complete with loading gauge, but such was the tightness of the curve that locomotives were banned from using it, necessitating shunting being done by a minimum length of goods train! The siding was removed and the ground frame closed on 1 August 1937. Elsewhere, at the station site itself – finally closed to passengers from 28 September 1924 – little has changed except that there is still a gas lamp at this stage, there are basic seats underneath the awning and, somewhat incredibly for such a small and relatively unimportant station, once more 'You may TELEPHONE from here'! Note the total absence of signals here to protect trains. The station approach road comes in from the bottom left. After the First World War only one daily down passenger train called at the station!

In October 2002 the site is much tidier and most definitely looks 'lived in'. The volunteers on the Swindon & Cricklade Railway have made great strides in creating a base here and restoring a railway presence so close to the heart of Brunel's Swindon – see the final section of this book for further images. *Mowat collection, Neville Bridger collection/MJS*

Above This slightly later view of the same scene is dated around 1937. Again, there appear to have been no changes, but on closer inspection a water butt has been added to the far end of the station building and, interestingly, a white-coated figure lurks in the doorway with a small parcels trolley! Elsewhere, the landscape, 273 feet above sea level, is as before, with farming pursuing its annual course with no regard to the railway. *Neville Bridger collection*

Below A little under 2 miles south of Blunsdon was Moredon Milk Platform, a 40-foot-long, 15-foot-wide structure situated on the northern edge of Swindon and opened on 25 March 1913 specifically for milk traffic. In 1923 a loop line was added, which from 1928 was used to access the nearby power station. This is the view in 1934, nearly two years after final closure on 1 October 1932; the 1914 sleeper-built platform hut has gone, but the wooden steps to the trackbed still look in fine shape. An intriguing-looking wooden – gauging? – structure hangs on the wall of the Pinehurst-Lydiard Millicent road overbridge, next to the 35 milepost, while in the distance the track curves sharply westwards on its way to Swindon. The point blade on the extreme left marks the start of the power station turnout. *MJS collection*

66

Rushey Platt

Right Of all the locations on the stretch of line covered by this book, Rushey Platt was perhaps the most unusual. Originally a terminus ending in a field, in February 1882, and by 1885 boasting two stations with four platforms, it served virtually no locale, being situated on an isolated edge of Swindon, just west of the massive GWR Works complex! The M&SWJR line crossed the GWR at this point, with one station being immediately to the south of this bridge and the other on a spur that swung eastwards to join the GWR and which was the originally intended route for the railway to terminate at the GWR's Junction station. This westwards view in September 1973

shows the M&SWJR route approaching the Rushey Platt area and crossing the original A420 Swindon-Wootton Bassett road. Oh, that the roads were so quiet today, when the same scene is now dual carriageway approaching the Great Western Way 'racetrack'! *Neville Bridger collection*

Below The same road is now at the foot of the picture, with the bridge to the photographer's right. On the horizon is the embankment that carried the M&SWJR over the road and the main former GWR Bristol-London route. On the latter an ex-GWR 'Castle' Class loco, with a good head of steam, approaches Swindon on an up express on 9 April 1961 – sadly the details are not recorded. The chord line between the two railways can be seen curving away to the left, past the attractive triple signal gantry. Note the easy access to the lineside at this time, courtesy of a simple gate and footpath, a world away from the Health & Safety-obsessed railway of the 21st century. This view is totally unrecognisable now, as the site has been completely redeveloped as an industrial site, with even the embankment flattened and landscaped into oblivion. *John Spencer Gilks*

Left The unusual arrangement of station facilities is well shown in this 1934 view, looking north. The double track in the foreground is the M&SWJR route, on a falling gradient of 1 in 82, with the line to the GWR just glimpsed on the right, at a slightly lower level. As can be seen, the M&SWJR station is formed of two extremely short platforms, without waiting shelters or proper platform surfaces, having been reduced to this 25-foot length around 1917. Fred Adams, the signalman in the 1917-vintage 20ft by 14ft box controlling both passage along the line and access to the GWR, casually watches the photographer, arm resting on window frame. Note the goods wagons in a siding by the GWR chord, and that there seems to have been some reballasting on both sets of lines. After little initial traffic, milk did become important, as did a timber yard that was established adjacent to the lower-level station, but passenger traffic never grew, and was withdrawn officially from 1 October 1905. Freight continued until 19 May 1964, but the signal box stayed open until 14 June 1965, and a single line on the connection until 1975. The 'main line' track – to the left – between Swindon Town station and Moredon Power Station, was finally lifted in the last months of 1978, thereby at a stroke aborting any plans the new S&CR had of restoring this piece of history. *Neville Bridger collection*

Below left On the same day the lower-level station building is seen in more detail, complete with cycle casually awaiting the return of its owner. In the same style as many further north on the route, there is evidence in the wall immediately past the bike that three doorways have been bricked up, which, together with the wooden and lattice fencing, gives the impression that the building is now more home than station. The sidings to the goods yard are accessed immediately past the platform end, and the M&SWJR bridge over the GWR can be seen in the middle distance. *Neville Bridger collection*

The RCTS 'East Midlander' railtour of 6 May 1956, already seen at several locations, has now reached Rushey Platt. The crew of train engine No 40454 prepare to climb back aboard, watched by the fascinated onlookers in the first two coaches, while the fireman of the pilot, No 40489, leans on his cabside enjoying having his photograph taken for posterity. In the right background rakes of wagons stand by the GWR main line and one of Swindon's large factories of this period dominates the skyline. *John Edgington*

Swindon Town

Left The railway from the Rushey Platt direction reached Swindon Town station via a winding route, picking its way in cuttings around the hill of Old Town and finally arriving at the station site by making a sharp turn under the A361, Devizes Road. There was a rising gradient from Rushey Platt of 1 in 75/90, leading to the site 441 feet above sea level, one of the higher stations on our route. This undated view from before the First World War shows the view post-1905 when the station was remodelled and rebuilt and the large retaining wall was constructed. What looks to be one of the handsome 4-4-0 locos introduced by the M&SWJR in 1905 stands at the head of an up train. Carriage doors stand open, while intending passengers gather in small knots, possibly saying farewell to relatives and friends. Meanwhile, the fireman attends to some item on the loco's running plate as the engine itself expels unwanted steam. Goods wagons stand in the distance and in the sidings to the right of the station, with a tantalising glimpse of the turntable by the large retaining wall on the right. *Neville Bridger collection*

Below left Some half-century later a young Peter Townsend stood on tiptoe to capture what may have been his first railway picture, showing the same view in August 1959, just two years before the end of passenger services. The station starter signal gantry has lost one semaphore arm; a new gantry has sprouted by the turntable; the platforms have gained white edging; gas lamps have been replaced by more modern equipment; and the trees and grass have grown to colonise the right-hand retaining wall. *Peter Townsend*

The twin retaining walls survive in October 2002, together with the serpentine approach and access route to the station site, now as a footpath into an industrial estate (seen to the left in this view). The whole ambience is now much changed, however, with the rampant growth both on the right wall and on the ground, together with the redeveloped area and industrial units. *MJS*

A signpost marks the entrance to the footpath from the old station site, together with a mural that incorporates images from Swindon and its railway past. The locomotive depicted is No 6000 *King George V* and the building the Mechanics Institute – most definitely Great Western rather than the more appropriate M&SWJR! – while the post points to 'Lydiard Country Park', 'Old Town Rail Path' and 'Mouldon Hill'. The industrial unit is contained within the wire compound to the left. *MJS*

71

While the M&SWJR did not have the proliferation in either number or variety of motive power enjoyed by its neighbour the GWR, it did possess its own locomotives and three examples are here captured at Swindon Town on 30 April 1921 by renowned photographer A. W. Croughton.

The first, seen in her final years, is No 9, a 4-4-0 built in 1893 by Dübs & Co of Glasgow. It is here seen 'parked' in a sylvan setting beside the two-road engine shed. Note the original stovepipe chimney now with a cast-iron cap, and the loco's immaculate condition, with polished brass strip around the edge of the driving wheel splasher and burnished buffers – ready to work some special train? Allocated the number 1127 by the GWR, it was withdrawn in January 1924.

By comparison, No 11, a 2-4-0, was built in 1894, as recorded by the cab numberplate, which also declares the M&SWJR parentage, as does the magnificent script lettering on the tender. Although obviously in everyday use – witness the crew and two shunters complete with poles posing for their portrait – the loco is again in very clean condition. Note the outside spring above the leading axle, the addition of coal rails on the tender and the diamond-shaped Dübs builder's plate on the gilded splasher. Originally emerging from the Glasgow Works with a stovepipe chimney, this has again been changed to a cast-iron capuchon cap, fitted in 1902. Renumbered 1335 by the GWR, it survived to serve BR, finally giving up the ghost in September 1952, together with No 1334 (ex-M&SWJR No 10); No 1336 (ex-No 12) remained until March 1954.

No 26, an 0-6-0 at the head of a mixed freight train, is again clean and adorned with gilding to the splasher, which doubles as a maker's plate; note also the script on the tender and the raised numerals on the cabside, but this time as individual numbers. In contrast to the above locos, Nos 19-28 were constructed by Beyer Peacock of Manchester, beginning in August 1899 for 19-24 and August/September 1902 for the rest. No 26 left the Works in the last week of August, was renumbered 1010 by the GWR at the 1923 Grouping, was rebuilt with a Belpaire firebox and taper boiler in October 1926, and finally withdrawn in December 1934, after running 179,491 miles. *All Neville Bridger collection*

Rush-hour at Town station! Pausing by the starter signal gantry is quite probably the most modern passenger traction ever seen on the route, in the form of 'Standard' No 76063, taking water before restarting a four-coach Southampton-Cheltenham St James service. Although undated, the view is post-August 1956, when the locomotive was introduced to traffic, and most likely in the late 1950s, partly judging by the apparel of those on the platform and the presence of an ex-GWR 0-6-0PT and two coaches at the far end of the right-hand platform, providing a connection to Junction station, the actual working of which is unknown. The up platform was 528 feet in length, while the down one was 18 feet shorter. Note the check-rail in the foreground on a not particularly tight curve!

How the mighty are fallen! Yes, this is the same aspect, seen in October 2002. The only clue here was provided for the photographer, who traversed the slope delineated by the trees on the left to gain access to the site by the route that had previously reached the station building. Although partly disguised by the sprout of industrial units, the line of the roadway roughly mirrors the old trackbed. *R. K. Blencowe collection, Neville Bridger collection/MJS*

One permanent feature of the 'past' views at Town station is the footbridge, linking the two platforms and spanning the main running lines. In the first, undated, view, which is probably shortly after remodelling, an unidentified tank engine moves through the up platform with two box vans, watched by a member of the station staff. The footbridge was a relatively simple affair, erected in 1885, comprising a steel skeleton lined with wooden planks and with no cover for passengers crossing in inclement weather! Initially produced as a postcard, the angle of this image provides a rare panorama, showing on the left the entrance to the platform, its garden and posters, and the repeater semaphore close by the footbridge pier. To the right there is a wealth of activity, with two lines occupied by freight – and wooden steps giving access to one of the wagons from the platform – and more goods wagons in the distant sidings. There do not appear to be many passengers waiting on the down platform, but a large bag sits blatantly on the white edging.

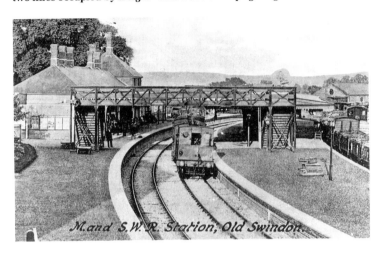

Forward to 25 March 1956, and there are subtle changes. The footbridge has gained lamps with stylish surrounds and the marks from countless blasts from locomotive chimneys; it has also gained a large sign advising passengers to 'Change here for Swindon Junction…' and other destinations. The station garden is still there, but the posters have all gone, as has the signal by the bridge; a television aerial has sprouted from the tall station building chimney; the amount of freight present is much reduced; and the up platform has had some ad hoc repairs.

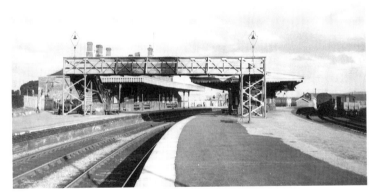

Finally, around the late-1950s/early '60s the lamps have lost their appendages and the platform resurfacing has now mellowed with time. No 31619 pauses at the head of a Southampton-Cheltenham service, watched by a single onlooker – Harry Grenside – as passengers prepare to board. The sidings to the right are now empty. *Neville Bridger collection/Terry Gough/Alan Lillywhite, John Spencer Gilks collection*

These two views use the footbridge as a vantage point. In the first, on a bright and sunny 24 September 1956, No 9605 runs north through the station. Allocated to 82C (Swindon) shed at this time, it has no doubt been involved in shunting duties in and around the station and is now returning to its home, by way of the Rushey Platt spur. This angle shows the low L&SWR-design 'A' signal box at the platform end – provided with 17 levers in 1904, to replace the original, during the station remodelling – the signals it controls, the water column and, just discernible by the box steps, the token catcher. Also seen are the deep retaining walls and the bridge supporting the Devizes Road. Prior to the 1904/5 remodelling, the station boasted three tracks through the station, although the middle one was merely for run-round purposes. On rebuilding, the up platform was built out slightly and the down was extended both in length and width, leaving space for just the two tracks seen here. To 'compensate', a through road was provided on the west side of the up platform, effectively turning it into a true island platform. New waiting rooms were provided on this platform at the same time. *R. M. Casserley*

On a much dirtier day, a 'U' Class loco restarts its southerly journey with a typical three-coach train to Southampton, as the disgorged passengers prepare to brave the elements outside the station. Note how the rural aspect of the top view opposite is here tempered by the loss of trees behind the station building and the appearance of houses beyond the train. Note also the Hawksworth coach at the rear of the train. *David Lawrence, Hugh Davies collection*

Above The actual Town station building was rarely photographed other than as an incidental. Here, however, an unknown photographer has seen fit to record the admittedly solid and somewhat ugly building for posterity. On yet another wet day, it is a case of one out and two in as regards visitors, with evidence of a further presence in the bicycle resting against the wall. A solitary poster board remains by the entrance to the platform, although the wooden supports of another remain on the wall. The carriage of a train can just be glimpsed in the platform. The relatively wealthy presence of the clean Austin and Standard, registered to Wiltshire and Gloucestershire respectively, presumably means their travellers will not have the long walk into town! Passenger services were withdrawn with the rest of the route in September 1961, but the station stayed open for goods traffic until 19 May 1964. Coal traffic ceased on 3 November 1966, followed by the Esso Oil traffic late in 1968. Thereafter, much of the site was cleared, but amazingly the up line was re-instated in 1970 for the site to become a railhead in connection with the building of the M4 motorway! The reprieve was short-lived, however, and tracks were finally lifted from Moredon to Town in 1978. *Neville Bridger collection*

Opposite page On a bright summer's day in June 1956 the photographer has captured the waiting area on the two main platforms, framed by the footbridge, as a train disappears towards Southampton. Discernible in the shadows are all the trappings of a traditional British Railways station – toilets, cloak room, newsagents, refreshment room, weighing machine, posters and notices, bench seating, and yet another bicycle leaning against the wall. On the seat a young person looks at her luggage, legs tucked beneath her – with no one else on the platform, has she been abandoned?

Once more it seems incredible that this view in October 2002 is the same place, but so it is. Broadly taking the line of the platforms, the old trackbed becomes the roadway, with perhaps the only inkling of the location being the distinct curve in the road mirroring the line of the railway. *Neville Bridger collection/MJS*

London and South Western Ry.
———
787
TO
SWINDON TOWN
Via ANDOVER JUNCTION.

Turning through 180 degrees from the previous views, but retaining the footbridge as a frame, No 5350 is seen three months earlier, on 25 March 1956, arriving with a Swindon Junction-Andover service, with the usual B Set coaches augmented by a parcels van bringing up the rear. Accentuated by the angle of light, the engine looks in creditably clean state. To the right the large signboard reads, 'Change here for Swindon Junction Bath Bristol and South Wales Didcot Oxford Reading and Paddington' – talk about spreading your net wide! Any prospective travellers to these destinations, however, would have a fairly lengthy and not straightforward walk to reach the Junction station to make connections, unless they waited for a connecting 'shuttle' train (see page 82). Note the jumble of buildings above the coaches, some ramshackle, but one with distinctly ecclesiastical windows – this was the M&SWJR General Offices from the opening of the railway to Swindon in 1881.

Today the roofline in the background is as before and the 'ecclesiastical' building remains, but with windows now replaced with more modern ones. Prior to the 1950s this element of the railway's General Offices – closed as such in 1924 – had an extra dimension to the left of the building in this view. The ramshackle appendages have also been swept away. While the roadway appears to be following the curvature of the old rails, they would actually have passed through the left-hand unit, aiming for a point between the trees and housing beyond. The area now most definitely does not have the ambience of yore! *Terry Gough/MJS*

In the first of these three undated views of the platforms and their surroundings we are standing on the west side of the up island platform, providing a rare glimpse of the 55-foot turntable provided in the 1904 remodelling, which necessitated part of the embankment behind it being excavated. Signs by the turntable urge: 'Notice. Caution. Remove no slide till table is stopped dead' – perhaps something to do with the locking mechanism? Note the ground signal controlling the exit from the sidings, which converge on the bridge beyond the end of the platform, the wealth of semaphores and the background buildings – including the remains of the General Offices – seen in greater detail.

The second view shows the width of the post-1905 island and the provision afforded at Town station, clearly to accommodate anticipated enhanced levels of traffic and to give waiting passengers full protection from the elements. A Cheltenham-bound train stands in the main platform, while on the left an ex-GWR '63XX' 2-6-0 waits for the road with a northbound train of empties.

Finally, on the down platform we have a better view of the waiting area on the opposite platform, together with a second look at the facilities on this one. In what is thought to be a later photograph than the top view, there have been landscaping developments behind the distant signal box and the provision of a starter signal on this platform for up trains. *Neville Bridger collection (2)/MJS collection*

While in other respects this view is contemporary with that seen on the previous page – the provision of a television aerial on the station building gives some clue – the starter signal previously seen is absent here. On this damp day travellers are beginning to gather, so presumably a train is due.

Again, the skyline and the two prominent houses, right of centre, link the two views, but the detritus of modern industrial sites is no match for the aesthetics of yesteryear! *Neville Bridger collection/MJS*

Judging by the overturned barrel and the position of the puddle in the foreground, this rare unimpeded view south from Town station was taken on the same day as that opposite; presumably the photographer has snapped the view from beneath the station canopy before venturing out to take the shot already seen. The curvature of the track leaving the station is well evidenced here, as is the siding to the sheet repairing shed and permanent way hut on the extreme right. In the middle distance stands the elegant goods shed, erected after the First World War on the site of the original, passed by the short siding to the cattle-pen bay. In the middle distance, just beyond the goods shed, the various running lines and sidings come together to cross the Evelyn Street bridge, thereafter to further converge into the two running lines to the south, past the engine shed that served the railway until 1924. Note the matter-of-fact station nameboard, matching those at the northern end.

In 2002 we see more of the industrial units and the road this time utilising the former trackbed to provide road access to the site. The wheelie-bin has replaced the oil drum! *Neville Bridger collection/MJS*

Motive power at Town station was either ex-GWR or ex-SR, with the latter handling the lion's share of the through services between Southampton and Cheltenham and the former either freight, local shunting or the shuttle service between here and Junction station. One such shuttle is seen behind No 7741 (NB23937/30) on a bitterly cold 6 December 1952, having arrived with the 11.13am from Junction. Somewhat strangely, the locomotive bears an 85B (Gloucester Horton Road) shedplate, rather than a more normal Swindon version; perhaps Swindon depot had 'borrowed' it and pressed it into service for some reason. It remained a Gloucester locomotive until 30 December 1961, when it was sold to London Transport, becoming LTE No 96. Notice how the snow has been well trodden on the down platform and is cleared from the edge, whereas where the photographer is standing the snow lays undisturbed; even on the tracks closest to the camera there appears to have been little or no removal. Note also the 'GWR' legend still visible on the tank side, almost five years after Nationalisation, and the lamp headcode, indicating a branch passenger train. *Hugh Ballantyne*

Our final train at Town, yet another Cheltenham-Southampton turn, is behind No 31619 on 5 March 1960. With a mixture of coaching and van stock behind his train, the driver takes a few moments before departure to enjoy the afternoon sunshine and attend to a little preventative oiling, watched by a solitary passenger from the first coach. The loco is seen again from the cattle dock, with the gap for the short siding in the foreground. The plain station nameboard is shown again to great effect, together with a rake of 16-ton mineral wagons and an unusual view of the nearby housing. The photographer's briefcase rests against the post on the extreme right. *Both Gerald Adams*

A last look back: on 24 September 1956 the station site is set out in all its glory, sitting squat and surrounded by housing, much of it at a higher level. The aforementioned short down siding is seen in greater detail here, as is the land to its right leading up to the station building and approach road. On the extreme left of the picture stands the 1912 water tower, no doubt the supply for the platform-end column. A serviceman partakes of the sunshine on the platform, while at the other end three station staff look towards the photographer. Just short of 30 miles from Andoversford, we have another 18 to go to Marlborough.

After the end of all traffic on the line, demolition of Swindon Town station was not long in coming. This is the view in the very early years of the 1980s, when the Engineering Department of the nascent Swindon & Cricklade Railway had descended on the site to recover redundant platform edging. Note how tree growth is already disguising the site. The old General Offices still stand, but with windows boarded up; by 2002 they had been renovated and become home to a firm of Chartered Accountants.

Once more, the outline of housing in the distance echoes the earlier view and the roadway mimics the tracks, albeit not on exactly the same piece of ground. As both north and south of this site is still accessible as a walkway, it is a shame that some semblance of the old infrastructure was not retained. *R. M. Casserley/Reg Palk/MJS*

Chiseldon

A delightful and tranquil view of Chiseldon station on 15 August 1954, looking towards Marlborough. The 3 miles from Swindon Town were broadly in a south-easterly direction, skirting around the eastern edge of Burderop Wood, then following the local contours before arriving on a south to south-east curve. The level of provision for staff, passengers and traffic at even small country stations is well exemplified in this photograph, with the substantial signal box and goods store, parcels office and main building. Note the fairly steep access to the station, seen between the box and the smaller building to the left, and the proliferation of poster boards. Could it be that the railway anticipated locals having to wait for long periods, thus needing something to read? *Norman Simmons, Hugh Davies collection*

CHISELDON, SHOWING THE CHURCH.

As can be seen from this early-20th-century photograph, the sweep of the 1 in 300 climb on the northern approach was through a deep cutting. Seen from high up on the approach path, the original, narrow, wooden 1881 signal box dominates the view, partly obscuring the houses and goods yard beyond. In the latter, twin sidings hold wagons waiting to be loaded and unloaded, the one nearest the running line having a loading gauge despite being barely long enough to hold any length of train! As the main line heads for the cutting in the distance, a trailing siding, installed around 1905, joins on the up side, to run into a 275-foot horse dock behind the main platform on the left, which here contains horse boxes for the nearby training stables.

As has been seen so many times already in this collection, the present-day views bare little or no resemblance to the earlier ones, but at least here, in October 2002, the aspect is still pleasant, being a green area unsullied by either road or industrial development. The two houses on the right are common to both shots, although the right-hand one has been extended and improved over the years and the other has lost its thatch, replaced by modern tiles. Note how the cutting has been disguised by verdant growth over the years. *Neville Bridger collection/MJS*

The first of these three views from the up platform dates from between 1915, when the parcels office was provided, and 1920, when a goods store was built next to the signal box. The station looks prosperous and a hive of activity; on the down platform two men roll and organise barrels – presumably from the nearby Elm Tree

public house, by the tree on the left, and no doubt using the cart just glimpsed in the left-hand bay – and there are more barrels and a number of milk churns on the up platform, together with a handful of people, young and old, presumably waiting for a train. The original signal box is to the right and, with the original wooden platform facings here replaced by brick and part of the surfaces now asphalted, the whole scene oozes charm, peace and quiet affluence.

In the 1950s the railway is still operating, but there is a subtle shift in ambience. The Elm Tree has lost its big tree, the tall down platform semaphore has gone, there is a new 12ft by 12ft 20-lever signal box constructed in 1942, and the platform surface looks in need of attention. Elsewhere, rails lie in the 'four-foot', presumably awaiting collection.

Today the pub still stands – note the roof outline common to all three views – the slope down from the road that once crossed the railway by the bridge is still evident, and trees still proliferate on the right, but otherwise it is difficult to imagine that a railway once ran here. Again, however, the station area is green and pleasant!

Neville Bridger collection (2)/MJS

Standing under the lea of the road bridge seen in previous views and looking back towards Swindon, No 6334 is captured on 15 March 1958 during a period of shunting. A shunter looks towards the loco's cab, while a companion, coupling pole under his arm, can just be seen to the right of the engine, waiting at the rear of the train. The signalman in his box watches the action. The rudimentary waiting shelter on the down platform – half of which was converted into a 'lock-up' around 1920 – is temporarily empty, while the equally plain and matter-of-fact station nameboard on the left, echoing the style seen at Swindon, announces the location. No 6334 had been a Swindon (82C) locomotive for four months at this date and would remain so until withdrawal on 18 April 1959.

The wall by the nameboard survives in October 2002, but now anyone surveying the scene is much closer to its top, due to the landscaping that has filled in the previous gulf between the road bridge and trackbed. Partially masked by the tree growth on the left, the area now hardly looks large enough to have accommodated the station and sidings of yore. *H. C. Casserley/MJS*

In railway photographs, as with so many other facets of life, appearances can often be deceptive. Seen on 8 September 1961, again looking back towards Swindon, but this time from the down platform, Chiseldon station looks the epitome of quiet confidence and permanence, but the end is only three days away. Posters and timetables adorn both station and goods office buildings in the bright late-summer sunshine, a box van stands in the far siding awaiting collection, and the signalman stands by his window, his door open to the balmy elements. The entrance to the platform can be seen to the left of the signal box, with the fencing of the access path seen climbing up from there past the main building. The main station veranda was renewed in 1917, when the front valance was reduced in height, leading to the angular cut-off on the side elevation. *Neville Bridger collection*

A mile or so south, Chiseldon Camp Halt served the military camp near the tiny village of Draycott Foliat. At 526 feet above sea level, it opened on 1 December 1930, although the camp had been served by a loop to the main running line since September 1914. As can be seen here on 8 September 1961, again three days before closure, it was a small, low, wooden affair amidst a flat, open landscape, hard by the A345 Swindon-Marlborough road, then a relatively quiet former Roman road, but nowadays a very busy arterial quasi-trunk road between the two locations. A dead straight, single-track line saw few trains stopping here, with its small shelter, open to wind and weather, and two low-powered lamps.

In October 2002 the footpath gives an approximation of the trackbed, providing at least some semblance of a railway memory. The road is now shielded from view by growth in vegetation, while out of sight to the right what was once the easterly reaches of the camp site is now a semi-official gypsy encampment, with the old access roads totally disguised by substantial earth movements. *Neville Bridger collection/MJS*

Ogbourne

Both road and railway from just south of Chiseldon, past the Camp Halt and as far as Ogbourne, ran in virtually a dead straight line and no doubt there were occasions when trains would race the tarmac competitors. Whether No 31639 had such a challenge is unknown as it runs into Ogbourne station on 25 June 1958 with the 2.00pm Cheltenham Lansdown-Southampton standard three-coach service; the competing road is just behind the huts on the right. In the left distance an ex-GWR '63XX' 2-6-0 stands by the signal box – the roof of which can just be seen above the last coach – waiting for the token for the single track stretch north to Swindon. Note the gentle rolling hills of Round Hill Downs on the right, a strong feature of this area of the route. Like so many of the smaller stations on the line, the facilities at Ogbourne were divorced from the hamlet served, this time by around half a mile. Much closer was – and still is – a golf course that was immediately across the A345 road. *John Spencer Gilks*

Above Moving to the 246-foot down platform and looking south towards Marlborough around 1930, this delightful period shot shows an unidentified GWR 'Duke' Class 4-4-0 with a large curved nameplate heading northwards off the single track into the station loop with a truly mixed goods train. As the driver leans out of his cab, the scene is full of atmosphere, with the delicate tracery of the lamp bracket, the 'house-style' station nameboard, corrugated iron waiting shelter, signal box and squat main building, complete with a trio of fire buckets, all provided new with the opening of the station in 1881. The only real change from then is the shortening of the massive main building chimney, which originally stood approximately the same height as the building! The signal box, with a new brick base provided in 1914, is probably painted chocolate and buff with white window frames. *Neville Bridger collection*

Below Thirty years or so later, although the shelter, canopy and signal box have obviously received a lick of paint, the buckets remain (respectively marked 'GWR', 'BR' and 'BR(W)'), and the trees still give a rural aspect to the scene, the 'feel' has changed. Gone are the attractive lamps, the well-tended garden on this platform and the posters on the up shelter, the signal box telegraph pole has been replaced with a slightly shorter version, and the down platform has been resurfaced beyond the building, together with losing the earlier fencing. The signal box is now only in use as a permanent way office, replaced by one behind the photographer. *Neville Bridger collection*

The passage of time has wrought further change at the station. In an undated view, but obviously after the end, Ogbourne has now lost its signal box, with an attendant encroachment of tree growth onto the platform; grass is making a claim on the trackbed between the sleepers; the fire buckets and seats have gone; and although the down siding still remains at the far end of the platform, the whole is pervaded by an air of impending dereliction.

Of all the places visited in the preparation of this book, Ogbourne in 2002 was probably the hardest to track down positively and the least satisfying in comparison with the past views. Incredible as it might seem, this is the same place! The bushes to the right very roughly mark the outline of the old up platform, but only by virtue of the raised ground giving the clue to the past facility, while the way into the light here, albeit along the old trackbed, will not lead peacefully to Marlborough, but rather on to the busy A345! *Neville Bridger collection/MJS*

Above Looking north from the up platform, a slightly unusual class of motive power for the line is seen on 7 July 1958, as No 3203 heads south with a through freight, complete with appropriate lamp headcode. The station, with its somewhat drunken chimney-pot, is obviously open for business, with a prospective passenger and luggage on the two platform seats and the photographer's car temporarily parked outside. Note the A345 on the right, with the speed de-restriction sign, and Round Hill Downs in the background. *David Lawrence, Hugh Davies collection*

Below Just three years later, on 8 September 1961, a box van stands in the short bay on the right, the two signal boxes are still in situ, although the view of the nearer one is rather restricted, and that chimney pot has been decapitated! A mere three days from closure, both tracks seem to have seen some recent reballasting. Note the change in level of the down platform, to accommodate the loading of cattle and milk churns, and in the distance the 1943-vintage signal box that was provided courtesy of American troops, when the up loop was extended and control of the signals and points was transferred from the original platform box. *Neville Bridger collection*

These tree views were taken from the south end of the down platform. The first is another delightful and evocatively attractive view, from around 1930. The signalman stands at the top of the stairs to his box for his portrait to be captured, while on the platforms milk churns await collection and, on this side, a wonderful period tractor, with solid wheels and no cab – newly delivered via the end loading dock? – shows what sort of machinery farmers used to have to deal with. Yet another decorative lamp stands just beyond the tractor and, in the distance, the new down-side signal box has not yet been built, but we have the first glimpse of an access path to the up platform from the top of the well-trimmed embankment – a short-cut from the north end of the village? There is also neat fencing marking the station limits on the embankments on both sides of the track.

Thirty-odd years later the end is most definitely here. Gone are the platform signal box, station seating, lighting and posters, together with the fencing and access seen above. The 1943 signal box is now in situ, but probably out of use at this juncture. Once more a sad sight compared to that above.

Again, the view today is deceptive. A clue to the location, though not readily apparent to the uninitiated, is the slight gap in the line of the left-hand bushes, which marks the spot where the old signal box stood! While some of the trackbed of the route covered in this book is accessible for walkers, it would be a brave person who attempted a stroll here. *Neville Bridger collection (2)/MJS*

Above On 24 September 1956 the 10.08am Cheltenham-Andover train pauses at Ogbourne, in the illustriou hands of No 7808 *Cookham Manor*. The station official at the foot of the signal box steps has a piece of paper i his hands – a message for the loco's driver? – and with a carriage door still open, he will have time to deliver i The ballast between the two tracks looks fresh and, with the mound of discarded sleepers in the right foregroun the permanent way men have presumably recently paid a visit. Elsewhere, the gates to the goods yard are firml closed and, beyond them, a high-sided van climbs the gradient towards Swindon on the A345. *H. C. Casserley*

Below Moving slightly further south, the photographer has 'trespassed' to take this wider view. Although th picture is undated, the neatness of the embankments in the distance, together with the previously seen fencin still in fine condition and the freight wagons to the right marked 'LMS', 'NE' and 'Baldwin', mean that it wa probably taken during the inter-war years. Milk churns once more grace the platforms, the ornate gas lamps stan ready to illuminate the station and the new signal box at the north end of the platforms has not yet been provide With the goods yard gate open, here is a station ready for business. *Neville Bridger collection*

Finally, looking south towards Marlborough on a dull and misty day around 1959, No 31619 arrives with an unusually short train of just two coaches. The driver looks out imperiously and not a little suspiciously at the photographer as his charge slows for the station, probably on an Andover-Swindon turn. Immediately to the right of the locomotive, chimneys of the village of Ogbourne can be dimly seen through the tops of the lineside bushes.

When the railway was in situ the A345 road veered away from the line by the station at Ogbourne to dive beneath the tracks before passing through the village and returning to the proximity of the railway on the other side. After closure, the highways authority, to iron out this 'kink' in the road, appropriated the short stretch of the trackbed that skirted the village. Thus, many thousands annually drive over the course of the old railway on what now seems to be a natural part of the roadway, most probably blissfully unaware of the significance of the stretch of tarmac. The view here is of the northern start to that stretch, with the curve echoing that from the sidings seen above. *Colin Caddy collection/MJS*

Marlborough

Above Marlborough, an ancient and important market town, was the third 'major' station on the route covered by this book, but although it may have come after Cirencester and Swindon in importance, it was certainly greater than those two in the aesthetic quality of its surroundings. Delightfully rural, as can be seen here, with the escarpment of Postern Hill in the background, the railway skirted to the east and south of the centre of the town, hugging the contours as it did so. On a beautifully sunny day around the late 1950s/early 1960s, No 31629 draws into the station on yet another Cheltenham-Southampton turn, with once again a member of the footplate crew keeping his eye on the photographer. On the left what looks as though it could be the fireman of the ex-GWR 0-6-0PT seen in the distance, with the light engine lamp headcode, walks away from us towards that loco. *Alan Lillywhite, John Spencer Gilks collection*

Opposite page This posed, period view is from a postcard that bears the legend 'This railway forms communication towards the south with Southampton and the Isle of Wight, and on the north joins the Midland Railway at Cheltenham.' An inexpensive piece of publicity – would that the line could offer such luxuries today! Dating from around 1912, an M&SWJR 4-4-0 locomotive can just be seen beyond the man on the left, about to run into the platform but seemingly ignored by the waiting throng, who are all more interested in having their photograph taken! The picture is full of delights, from the ancient grounded coach on the extreme right to the milk churns and enamel signs, period costumes, and the enormous trunk on the edge of the platform.

The Midland and South Western Junction Station, Marlborough.

This railway forms communication towards the south with Southampton and the Isle of Wight, and on the north joins the Midland Railway at Cheltenham.

A similar angle on 8 June 1954 shows No 6349 on an exception to the usual trains that we have seen on the route. Having paused alongside the 304-foot-long platform, the 2-6-0 restarts its B Set of twin coaches forming the 2.35pm Andover Junction-Swindon Town 'local'. From what can be seen, nothing has changed from the earlier view. Note the 'black house', as it was known locally, beyond the last coach; this was a pair of 'semis' that were occupied originally by Station Master and shunter and came to earn the soubriquet after the tarring of the exterior immediately before the First World War. Access to them was by way of a footpath from the up platform and across the A346 Andover road, the bridge parapet for which can just be discerned in the left distance.

The land occupied by the station has been the site of a newly developed Highways Depot for Wiltshire County Council since 1997; this is the comparative view in October 2002. The station approach, still climbing steeply from the Marlborough-Andover road, as it did during the time of the railway, can be seen entering the yard immediately to the left of the house roof on the right. *Neville Bridger collection/Hugh Ballantyne/MJS*

Just moments after the view of No 31629 on page 98 was taken, that train is at rest in the platform while on this side sister locomotive No 31619 enters the station with a train bound for Cheltenham. Note how here No 31619 wears a Southern-style disc as headcode, rather than the more usual lamp; on the SR this would have indicated, amongst others, a service from Eastleigh to Andover Junction, and one wonders whether someone had overlooked its replacement at the latter location, before the train began the journey up the ex-M&SWJR. With much of the route as single track, tight control of timings was essential for this type of train passing to work without undue delay to one of them. The large goods shed on the right was surpassed only by Swindon and Cirencester, and was built to anticipate a healthy level of traffic.

Once again, the depot site is seen from the appropriate angle. The left-hand railway boundary, just behind the platform fencing in the earlier photograph, is here delineated by the row of trees. *Alan Lillywhite, John Spencer Gilks collection/MJS*

With the rolling surrounding countryside attractively picked out by the summer sunshine of 1 September 1952, we see yet another variation in route diagram. Attached to a B Set comprising coaches 6348 and 6338, No 5510, with headcode lamp yet to be put into place, waits to form the 4.00pm shuttle to Savernake, interestingly utilising the up platform for a down service. Note the now ubiquitous 'house-style' of the station nameboard. This train was just one variation on the type of traffic handled at the station, which included schools trains for the local College, excursions for Savernake Forest, annual fair traffic, pigeon specials and horse boxes. The very last passenger service, nearly three years after normal service had been withdrawn, was a College train from Paddington, on 1 May 1964, hauled throughout by a 'Hymek' diesel. It was truly a dramatic end as the diesel ran off the end of the track, the driver not realising that the rails towards Ogbourne had been lifted!

Now with our back to the main highways site, we look to the growth of trees on Postern Hill, past the Kennet DC part of the site, with this part of the compound seemingly being used mainly for parking. *H. C. Casserley/MJS*

This undated view, probably from around the early 1960s, shows the view south from the station across the bridge over the A346 road to the 1933 GWR signal box and beyond. As with other stations on the route, one platform had all the main services, while the other made do with much sparser facilities; the rather plain and open corrugated iron structure on the down platform can be seen. When opened on 27 July 1881, the end of the down platform seen here was graced with a large brick-built water tower, but this fairly quickly became superfluous with supplies from elsewhere, and in 1917 was dismantled and transferred to Foss Cross. Although standing higher than the centre and most of the town it served, this station was almost universally known as 'Low Level', to distinguish it from its GWR neighbour, which stood on marginally higher ground, to the right in this view.

To have stood in the photographer's shoes for this comparison the view would have been a close-up of bricks! I have consequently stepped back a few yards to give a southerly aspect but to provide a little more for the viewer! The trees in the left background mark the boundary that was immediately behind the corrugated shelter above. *Neville Bridger collection/MJS*

Again looking south, but this time from the down platform, No 9721 is seen entering the station on 20 May 1961 with another B Set twin-coach train, the leading vehicle being W6228W. The train is unidentified, but could be an Andover Junction-Swindon 'local' or Savernake-Marlborough 'shuttle', probably the latter. The locomotive, though grimy, has had the 'new' British Railways logo cleaned on its tank side. The streaks on the smokebox indicate that perhaps not everything is watertight! A Swindon (82C) engine for the whole of its British Railways life, it was withdrawn on 16 June 1962. The appropriately named 'black house' mentioned earlier is seen in greater detail, and beyond it to the right the water tower at the High Level terminal station is just visible. To the left, another delightfully graceful bracket holds the gas lamp, while in the distance a somewhat strangely placed water column stands a little way from the station, requiring thirsty engines to stop short of the platform to satisfy their need!

When the railway was closed, the road bridge over which the train is passing was demolished and fencing put in place to protect the gap. It is now difficult to plot the previous crossing point on the ground, but with the help of a map of the highways depot this 'Washdown Area' is the current location. Not only has this railway disappeared, but so also has the other rail route into the town, and the 'black house' – all lost to development.
Mike Esau/MJS

With the late-afternoon sun casting long shadows, though by the dress and demeanour of the platform souls the temperature is still high, No 5367 pauses at Marlborough with the 6.30pm Swindon-Andover Junction service of 7 August 1950. Looking as though they have just crossed the somewhat primitive wooden barrow crossing in front of the train, the couple walking away from us have perhaps enjoyed a day out in Swindon. A trio rest outside the room signposted 'Refreshment Room & Teas' (added to the main building in 1884) below bunting and a Union Jack gaily blowing in the breeze – it would interesting to know the reason for the decorations. No 5367 was another Swindon locomotive at this juncture, but moved to Bristol (St Philip's Marsh) on 27 December 1952 and thence to Reading, from where it succumbed on 6 September 1958.

Sadly there is no bunting today, merely the 'back end' of the main building on the current site, with the right-hand boundary once more announced by the trees. At least the sun and shadows are common to both views! *John Edgington/MJS*

Above Viewed from across the A346 road bridge during what appears to be the late-1950s, No 6373 pauses with another Swindon-Andover Junction 'local' service, this time formed of ordinary non-corridor coaching stock rather than the more usual B Set. A man and his dog pay no heed to the train, while on the up platform a small girl stands at the door of what is now more simply called the 'Refreshment Room' – teas no longer served? A Royal Mail van waits in the station yard on the left, by the small wooden-gated entrance to the platform. Note the simple station nameboard positioned beyond the platform end, with no other signs visible to announce the location – if travellers missed it as their train entered the station, they could well wonder where they were! *Neville Bridger collection*

Below The caption on the reverse of this photograph simply says 'southbound goods', making no comment that the train is running 'wrong line'. As the date is 1 September 1952, the full route is still open, with both tracks in normal daily use. A possible reason could be that it has been held on the up line while a down passenger train passes, but another clue could be the 'pick-up goods' lamp code, which could indicate that the train has indeed picked up some items of rolling-stock from the up sidings at the far end of the station. Whatever the reason, the train is of mixed stock and vintage, hauled by No 6320 of Swindon, an elderly locomotive in fine external condition. Note the short horse-loading siding on the right. *H. C. Casserley*

The photographer has used the shallow embankment to the south of the station to capture this panorama in around 1930. The right-hand horsebox bears a 'GW' legend, while the Refreshment Rooms go one better, having their name emblazoned in tiles across the roof. A footpath from the road below accesses the horse dock on the right, while the path on the left leads to the 'black house', its garden and the High Level station. Sadly, the misty conditions over Postern Hill have prevented an ideal, peaceful rural vista.

Today the trees mark the gap created by the removal of the road bridge, and the building, together with others on the site of both stations, has been built in the last few years to totally obliterate the railway and the views across the valley. The footpath, however, remains as a secondary access to this house's garden. Many of the locals bemoan the passing of the railway. *Neville Bridger collection/MJS*

As a change from the limited variety of 'U' Class locomotives already seen, here No 31794 visits the route, unusually hauling a Swindon-Andover Junction train, on 30 July 1960. The front coach of the B Set is W6254W. A porter watches the departure from the distant platform, together with a solitary seated passenger complete with luggage. Note that the left foreground footpath has now become overgrown, due to the demise of the High Level station and the reduction in staffing at the M&SWJR station. As with other ex-SR locomotives on the route, No 31794 was an Eastleigh engine when captured for posterity, remaining at that shed until withdrawn on 22 July 1963. *Mike Esau*

Above To complete our journey along the old M&SWJR route, we take a brief comparative look at the architectural styles of the two Marlborough stations. The layouts of the two railways and their proximity are well exemplified in this view from around the late-1950s. The through route of the Low Level station and its short horse dock siding are seen clearly to the right, as is the 'black house', here taking pride of place in the centre. To the left is the old engine shed of the High Level terminus, together with the platform track and run-round facility. Judging by its condition, the shed has not been used for some time. *Neville Bridger collection*

Below As can be seen, the High Level station building was architecturally far more ornate than its more square and utilitarian neighbour. Opened in 1864, as broad gauge for the first ten years, it closed to passengers on March 1933, but saw out its centenary – just – with freight services finally being withdrawn on 19 May 1964. Though undated, it is obvious from this view that the building is no longer in use, its windows boarded up, fencing awry and the platform surface beginning to grass over – and the only occupant of the engine shed is a road lorry! Although this site has now been totally transformed by recent housing development, the semi-detached dwellings on either side of the station building are still extant, cheek-by-jowl with their newer brethren. *R. Simpson, MJS collection*

Preservation

The lifeblood for any preservation movement – apart from any paid staff – is a combination of volunteers and publicity. One good form of the latter, which at least spreads the message far and wide, is a railtour. In the days before economics gained a stranglehold over railway operations, supporters of the Swindon & Cricklade Railway affix an appropriate headboard to a Class 47 locomotive on Sunday 9 September 1979. Five hundred fare-paying passengers – including a healthy contingent from the local police! – enjoyed a day out to Paignton, leaving Swindon at 8.45am and arriving home 12½ hours later. It was planned to be 'the first of many', as it had been a good fundraiser, but sadly British Rail saw fit in 1980 to raise fares to the extent that a repeat was just not financially viable. Note the late and much-missed Ivor Huddy – then the Railway's volunteer Mechanical Engineer giving assistance on the right. *Reg Palk*

Top Volunteers on the chain gang. The work they do is vital to the survival of our private railway, imbuing them with enthusiasm, drive, ideas and – probably most important – free labour! On a summer Saturday around 1981, in obviously glorious summer conditions, the job of rock-breaking is overseen by the 'foreman' (right), preparing a trackbed at the the northern end of the Blunsdon site, with wagons already loaded with 'spoil' close at hand. Where are these 'youngsters' now? *Reg Palk*

Middle Some time later, and into late winter, more clothing is required, despite the exertions being undertaken. Looking towards Cricklade in the early 1980s, a permanent way gang work on the point at the north end of Blunsdon station. The ground frame box on the left at this time boasted an ex-Brecon & Merthyr three-lever frame, on loan from the photographer. *Reg Palk*

Bottom Just to prove that the men and boys don't always have it their own way – and, indeed, nor should they! – in 1982 Audrey Palk became the first lady fireman on the S&CR, having been passed out by an ex-BR Inspector on the Dean Forest Railway. She is seen here, the weekend after successfully completing the course, posing for the local press. Needless to say, on the

visible evidence, her skills will not be needed on this Kerr Stewart 0-4-0WT in the foreseeable future! Subsequent to this view, the loco, owned by Bill Parker, was moved to Bill's workshop in the Forest of Dean. *Reg Palk*

Opposite above Early days! Only months after the formation of the preservation society, volunteers are on the old trackbed at Blunsdon, beginning the long journey back to running trains. In the early months of 1979, shortly after gaining official access to the trackbed, Audrey Palk and two young stalwarts begin the serious and arduous task of plotting the route at the site of the old station, looking south, past the barbed wire and through the bridge towards Swindon. An early plan, intention, objective, hope was to 're-open part of the Midland & South Western Junction Railway, between Moredon Power Station and Cricklade'. Sadly, like so many before them, they were overtaken by events and competing interests, although something approaching this fine aim is still a possibility. *Reg Palk*

Opposite below Progress! A matter of months later, North Wilts District Council has given planning permission, Thamesdown Borough Council has agreed the lease, and track is laid on the main entrance to the

site, with sleepers laid ready for rails to be extended under the road bridge and into the old station site. At least a dozen volunteers – young and old and including Len Ponting (left) and Vince Comley (now a driver on the S&CR) – stand prepared for the work to come, including positioning the pile of ballast when the rails are fixed. The discarded farm gate had previously served to fence in a pony that grazed on the trackbed, preventing it from straying. *Reg Palk*

Turning through 180 degrees from the previous pictures, in 1980 the view northwards captures the emerging track in the right foreground and the construction of the ex-Black Bourton signal box cabin. Roughly positioned on the actual station site, this was the tantalising view for the enthusiastic preservationists, with rails and sleepers just waiting to be put into position! The original access road, seen on pages 64/65 sweeps in from the left foreground. Having your base – which inevitably involves a requirement for space for immediate needs, deliveries of large items and development – at a place that probably had the most restricted location on the old railway, called for much imagination in the forward thinking and planning. It is a credit to those involved over the past 25 years or so that by and large their aims have been fulfilled.

The same view is seen from the road overbridge in the spring of 1981 as the 'head of steel' progresses towards Cricklade while the signal box is taking shape, partially clad and roofed. Elsewhere, the main group concentrate on laying a concrete 'roadway' for better access to the right of the trackbed than that given by the rapidly decaying sleepers in the foreground. The signal box was eventually put into store, ready for use in due course at Mouldon Hill.

What a difference a day – well 20 years – makes! This is the same view in October 2002, showing just what can be achieved where there is vision and will. On a non-operational day, coaching stock stands in the new Blunsdon station, some 100 yards or so north of the original site. Now complete with facilities to safely accommodate the modern visiting public, the past is not forgotten – note on the left the grounded coach (now the First Aid and Training rooms) and the old lamp hut, now in use as an oil store. *Reg Palk (2)/MJS*

s mentioned earlier, any proposed railway preservation site has to have facilities for accepting delivery of large
tems, and this was achieved for the S&CR across the field on the far side of the pond seen here, as the old
1&SWJR station access was just not wide or uncomplicated enough. On a dry and sunny 18 May 1980, S&CR
upporter Cliff Vaisey arrives with a load of track panels, rescued from Rodbourne, Swindon. 'Doing their bit' for
he railway, the use of the lorry was donated by Mike Durham of SW Transport (Swindon) Ltd. As with volunteers,
uch assistance is meat and drink to private railways. The heavyweight Grove Allen crane, used to offload the
anels, stands in the background, waiting to pull forward to begin work.

Twenty years later the same scene is recorded on 12 March 2000. Note how the site has been fenced and
andscaped, and widened to accommodate the rather makeshift staff and café accommodation on the right. The
ormer greenery on the right has been cut back, but the sole tree between the pond and the trackbed has escaped
nd grown. The public entrance is now past this tree. Future development beckons in the centre distance, past
ne loco and coaching stock. *Reg Palk/MJS*

A further five months later there is movement – gone are the unsightly cabins, to make room for the transfer and transformation of the railway's two Norwegian coaches into café and staff accommodation. In this view on August 2000 they can be seen as the left-hand of the three rakes; the right-hand one is broadly in line with the old trackbed, which stretches into the distance, aiming for Swindon. Note the piles of sleepers, waiting to be used on the extension.

By 19 October 2002 there has been dramatic change. The Norwegian coaches, together with another, are now in place, and with the landscaping and paving make for a much more inviting and welcoming image for visitors. First impressions on arrival at a site are important, and these latest developments are certainly more likely to make people want to stay and spend money. In the middle distance, work is under way to prepare for the long-awaited 'break out', whereby the railway will strike forth southwards, over the River Ray bridge and on to the trackbed once more. In the foreground, Bob Simmons – one of the railway's oldest servants – casually strolls towards the station. *Both MJS*

Right The bridge that restricts the railway's southern escape from its present incarceration at Blunsdon spans the River Ray, and the way forward across it has been eyed with longing by the preservationists since the earliest days. Seen here on 22 January 1996, it certainly looks 'so near and yet so far'! The trackbed stretches out tantalisingly and seems to indicate that, apart from a 3-foot rise to the bridge bed from both sides, there is little that would hinder a rapid expansion of the S&CR system. *MJS*

Below When W. D. & H. O. Wills decided in 1980 to close the rail transport facility at their Colbourne Street, Swindon, factory, a substantial amount of equipment became available. Happily, much was donated to the S&CR, with probably the major

item being a 1953 40hp Fowler 0-4-0 diesel shunter (No 4210082) in full working order, together with a crate of spares. An immediate boon to the railway, it was subsequently repainted into a pleasing green livery and is seen here, several years later, at Blunsdon station, to be named (appropriately) *Woodbine*. The press are on hand for photographs and, at the far end of the platform, Majorettes are ready to perform. The great strides made by the relative handful of volunteers over the years since inheriting the site have already been commented on elsewhere, and are shown to good effect in this view of the much improved 'customer-friendly' facility. The signal box originated from Claydon Junction. *Reg Palk*

Below As with any railway restoration, in order to attract the public there is a need to go from somewhere to somewhere. Being 'in the middle of nowhere', stuck midway between the large conurbation of Swindon to the south and the ancient Saxon town of Cricklade (and the nearby Water Park) to the north, the railway has been up against it from the beginning. Having established its base at Blunsdon, it was necessary to aim for the next physical goal. This has been achieved at Hayes Knoll, around 1 mile to the north. Previously a 'greenfield' site, track was laid to the location in the early 1980s, with work then beginning on a platform to accept trains and passengers. As seen mid-decade, this structure is under way, with brickwork just about reaching platform height, while spare stock takes advantage of the space afforded by the second road. Already in position, at the platform end, is the railway's first 'home' signal – since replaced by a double gantry, controlling both roads. *Reg Palk*

Below To make the 'station' look the part, a signal box was required. As can be seen in this view on 20 June 1992, the partly erected structure – from Rowley Regis – positioned just to the north of the new terminus uses materials and a design that are true to the heritage aspect of the operations. Still not 100 per cent complete in 2003, it is, however, capable of controlling both ends of the station site and the adjacent shed yard. Ahead is yet another tantalising glimpse of what might be – the way to Cricklade and the north! *MJS*

As already mentioned, Hayes Knoll was not an M&SWJR location, but, like many former British Railways depots, the line's engine shed was to be adjacent to the new station, except that in this case the east wall of the shed would be the 'façade' of the station. Unlike other stations, however, that was all it would be – a façade – as, like a Hollywood set, it is merely a front with just the appearance of doorways, windows, etc. Anyone attempting to enter or look through these will be extremely unlucky! On 20 June 1992 the three-road shed – the first built for a 'new generation' preserved railway on a greenfield site – is taking shape, with the platform to the left, the roof in place and a healthy pile of sleepers on the right ready for use when required.

By 22 January 1996 things are really beginning to take shape, with the main outline of the platform complete – although the surface is yet to be put in place – some of the canopy area complete, and the shed now more weatherproof. Later developments saw the length of the covered accommodation extended towards the camera.

On 5 September 1999 the structure is seen in its extended state, open for business and taking on an authentic appearance. No 7903 *Foremarke Hall* stands temporarily parked outside for public viewing and publicity. Track is laid inside, with only the yard needing completion. In 1979 thoughts had been towards a second-hand affair, to contain costs for the young society – this all-new building must surely be preferable and well worth the wait. *All MJS*

Above No 7903, seen on the previous page outside the shed, is one of the long-term restoration projects being undertaken on the railway. As seen inside the shed on 12 March 2000, within the extension previously mentioned, appearances seem to indicate that the end is not far off, but this is deceptive, as there is still much to do. Emerging from Swindon Works in April 1949 – effectively a modification of a 40-year-old GWR design – under the auspices of the recently nationalised British Railways, *Foremarke Hall* went first to work at London's Old Oak Common shed. Thereafter there was only one change of abode, on 2 November 1963, when it was transferred to the other end of the London-South Wales route, to Cardiff East Dock. Withdrawal came not long after, on 20 July 1964, with an early move thereafter to Dai Woodham's infamous scrap yard at Barry Docks. Languishing there until 1981, it was rescued by Foremarke Hall Locomotive Ltd in June and moved to Blunsdon, stopping off briefly at Swindon Works Open Day en route on 5 June. *MJS*

Left Another long-term project is former Auto Coach 178. The property of Mike Little, it is here seen at the back of the shed on 5 September 1999, the working area roped off from the admiring public and with scaffolding erected to assist with restoration of the bodywork. Note the panelling and woodwork already completed at this end and along the bodyside. Hopefully complete by the summer of 2003, it will be finished to main-line standards and moved to a railway where it can 'stretch its legs' in company with Mike's '14XX' Auto Tank. *MJS*

Once more outside, work continues in 1996 to prepare the platform for public use, with the overall protecting canopy now in place, complete with 'S&C Rly' cast into the brackets in GWR style, but manufactured by Rover Group. Some of the multifarious types of rolling-stock are seen alongside, including a Fruit D closest to the camera. The attractive lamps along the wall were also made by Rover, and the mock windows and spaces for posters can be clearly seen. *Both MJS*

Another steam locomotive restoration project seen on the railway was that of ex-GWR 0-6-2T No 5637. Built in September 1925, again at Swindon Works, to a Collett design, it was the 28th of 200 locomotives constructed between December 1924 and October 1928. Working initially in South Wales and allocated to Abercynon depot from before the war to 10 September 1955, it then moved to Cardiff (Cathays), from where it made the short trip to Barry on 27 February 1960. Withdrawal came at that shed in the same week in July 1964 as *Foremarke Hall*, at which time it gained the distinction of being the last steam locomotive on Barry shed. Its move to the Barry Docks scrapyard to join No 7903 and the gathering horde of redundant engines was therefore only a short one. After a decade it made the journey to Tyseley for a proposed restoration, before being bought by Thamesdown Borough Council for restoration and use on the S&CR. It is seen here being carefully unloaded at Blunsdon in early April 1982, in the company of Ivor Huddy and Dave Titcombe. An official acceptance ceremony took place on 12 June of that year, with guests Councillor and Mrs Mike Bawden, the Mayor and Mayoress of Swindon.

Initial hopes were for restoration within three years, but due to there being no covered accommodation restoration had to be completed in the open, which did not help the timescale! In good weather on 24 May 1997 the boiler assembly is seen on the edge of the car park in Blunsdon yard, resting on an ex-Swindon Works boiler trolley, semi-naked but with a distinctly improved 'cared for' look.

Final restoration came in 2001, after which No 5637 was moved to the East Somerset Railway, to be given a chance to 'stretch its legs'. Initially outshopped from Blunsdon in green, the East Somerset Railway repainted it into unlined BR black during 2002. On 6 October, the first day of operation in its new livery, the locomotive stands in Cranmore station, waiting to haul the first train of the day to the other end of the line at Mendip Vale. With the skilful restoration of the station site, the whole has an authentic heritage look. *Reg Palk/MJS (2)*

We have seen No 7903 snug inside the shed at Hayes Knoll, but much work needs to be done outside, especially where heavy lifts are involved. On one such occasion, on 23 September 1996, the boiler is hung and swung in the Blunsdon yard, to position it for fixing to the newly fabricated ashpan. Paul Tomes, John Cruxon (7903 Society's Locomotive Manager ducking underneath) and Don Asher all take appropriate steps to finish the job and protect themselves! Three things soon become clear when working on railway engines – everything is heavy, everything is costly, and many things are beyond their use-by date – which means new builds, leading to new drawings or a search for old ones, and certainly leads to more expense. This is why so often the anticipated costs and dates for restoration are wildly inaccurate!

In two pieces again, but this time on the last lap. On 25 January 2003, boiler and frames are once more separated, but for the boilersmith to examine it before a final steam test is arranged and, hopefully, a final restoration to a working locomotive. The view is from the road overbridge at Blunsdon, with remedial work on the duckweed in the pond going on in the background. As this book was being prepared, the hope was for a return to service in time for S&CR's 25th Birthday celebrations in September 2003. *Both MJS*

Top Not yet quite ready to run, ex-GWR 2-8-0 heavy freight locomotive No 3845 is a recent arrival at Blunsdon on 11 February 1996, being one of a number of items of stock 'evicted' from their previous home in Brighton. Obviously the subject of a very long-term restoration, the previous robbing of many parts – not least a tender! – and having to stand out in the open at the S&CR will not help. Money and bodies are needed to see this fine locomotive hauling stock once more. Built as an aid to the war effort in April 1942, it was one of 83 '2884' Class of 'improved' 2-8-0s constructed over a 3½-year period from March 1938. Allocated to Reading and still there at the formation of British Railways in 1948, it moved to Southall on 4 October 1952 and Didcot on 16 May 1953. Subsequent wanderings took it to Wolverhampton and South Wales, before migrating back to the Midlands on November 1962, to Banbury shed, from where it was withdrawn – as with Nos 7903 and 5637 – on 20 July 196. Also like those two, it travelled to Barry Docks, where it rested and rusted until it was moved to the ill-fate Brighton Railway Museum in 1988 – the last tender engine to leave Barry. *MJS*

Middle While not what a lot of the public wish or expect to see at a preserved railway, diesels are often vital pieces of equipment, being both cheaper to operate and taking less time and effort to start up and put to bed at the end of the day. Former BR shunter No 03152 initially came to the railway in March 1984, the property of Bi Parker, having been despatched to the Swindon Works scrap line after withdrawal from Landore depot in South Wales in October 1983. Built at Swindon, as D2152, it entered service on 2 July 1960 at York, but within days was transferred east to Bradford (Hammerton Street). Duties were then in and around the North East until the move to South Wales in July 1974 after a major overhaul, which included a cut-down cab for restricted clearances in its new location. By that time it had been

renumbered under BR's TOPS system (in May 1974). A period in Swindon after 1988, shunting locomotives around what was hoped would become a museum was followed by a return to the S&CR. It is seen here in BR black livery, receiving some remedial attention and awaiting new injectors at Blunsdon on 18 August 1996, as Haydn Roberts prepares to fit a workplate. *MJS*

Bottom No 2022 is of the same '03' Class as 03152 above, but retains the original full-sized cab. Built at Swindon in May 1958 as D2022, its first allocation was at Immingham Docks on 14 June. Thereafter it worked in and around Lincolnshire until a reduction in local work saw it move north to Darlington in September 1980. Despite a relatively recent overhaul, its lack of train air brakes led to its withdrawal – from Gateshead, where it had been deployed as Newcastle station pilot – in November 1982. Sent to Swindon Works for scrapping on January 1983, it was rescued from there on 1 November by members of the S&CR. When built it had been allocated a steam series number of 11209, but this was never carried; neither was the current number and mock GWR brass cabside plate. Pictured here on 23 October 1989, in mock GWR lined green livery, it was on loan to the scrapyard of Cooper's (Metals) Ltd in Swindon, to replace their own failed shunter. Driver Ken Ramsden peers out of the cab for his portrait. *MJS, with permission*

Top Variety is the spice of life, and private railways are no exception. Visiting locomotives are a fillip for both the railway's own staff and volunteers, and the public. While 'big name' engines obviously cause the most stir, smaller ry can also create much interest. Such was the case during the visit of *Mirvale* to the S&CR in 1994. Seen at Blunsdon on 4 September, awaiting right of way into the station before beginning the day's work, the 1882-vintage

Hudswell Clarke 0-4-0ST was on loan from the Middleton Railway in Leeds. Like Ken Ramsden opposite, driver Brian Haines poses for his portrait. In the background is the ex-Central Clinic building from Islington Street, Swindon, donated in 1981 and serving then as café, booking office, staff accommodation, etc. *MJS*

Middle As a guest on the railway, ex-GWR 0-6-0PT No 9682 was a very special engine indeed. The subject of yet another long-term restoration project, when finally back in full steam it became the 100th locomotive to be restored from those rescued as rotting hulks from Dai Woodham's Barry Docks yard. With the main work undertaken at the private workshops within the old Swindon Works, it was moved to the S&CR for completion. It is seen in the yard outside Hayes Knoll shed on 12 March 2000, resplendent in brand new paintwork, on its first official day back in steam, cautiously moving about the yard to test the various moving parts before being trusted to the mile-long sprint to Blunsdon. New from Swindon on 31 May 1949, it was the last of 863 engines in the '5700' Class, which had begun life 20 years earlier! Initially at Tyseley depot, Birmingham, it moved to South Wales in July 1960, being finally allocated to Radyr (just north of Cardiff), from where the end came on 8 August 1965. A swift transfer to Barry Docks – one of 65 arrivals that year – was eventually followed by rescue in November 1982 and a trip to Southall, privately owned but under the auspices of the Southall Railway Centre. *MJS*

Bottom As well as small diesel shunters, the railway has provided a home in the past to larger beasts. In Blunsdon yard on 24 May 1997 is Sulzer Type 2 No 5222, newly returned from ARC (Southern) Ltd at Whatley Quarry having been on loan for the previous four or five years. New from BR's Derby Works in September 1963 as D5222, it was one of the last batch of the class to be built with original body styling, which included nose-end doors and bodyside ventilation grilles. After initial service at Cricklewood, it saw alternating use at the London end of both the Midland and West Coast Main Lines, finally leaving Cricklewood for Scotland (as 25072) in October 1976. Its sojourn north of the border ended in October 1982 with a move to Crewe, from where it was withdrawn in November 1985. Use as a training loco at Toton then followed, before Terry Bird of the S&CR bought it and moved it to Blunsdon on 18 March 1988. On the S&CR it was, like 2022, fitted with non-authentic brass cabside number plates. It was later sold on to RMS Locotec, and in 2003 was held in accommodation at Meldon Quarry, pending a decision on its future. *MJS*

Left The Rev Wilbert Awdry has a lot to answer for! Not only was he responsible for 'Thomas' and the amazing and continuing interest in and fascination for the character among children of all ages and nationalities, but also (although a little more indirectly!) for the young lady here celebrating her wedding day. On 25 July 1998 his granddaughter and her new husband 'pose' for photographs for the local press, alongside Gordon Titcombe as the Fat Controller with his red and green flags. *Thomas* looks mildly embarrassed, waiting patiently to take the newlyweds, just arrived from the church, to their reception at Hayes Knoll. Not the most common of venues for such an event, one might think, but as both were volunteers on the railway, it was most appropriate. With the weather and the event, a good time was had by all. *MJS*

Below Another happy event, but of a different kind – and in different weather – was the formal return to steam of *Slough Estates No 3*, seen here being ceremonially waved off at Blunsdon on 17 March 2001, as the banner is cut by Colin Benstead, a representative of Slough Estates, from whose private railway system the loco had come. Standing with him is Don Roberts, Chairman of the Slough & Windsor Railway Society, who had overseen the restoration. Onlookers brave the rain, as do the band, preparing to accompany the event with appropriate music. All ex-S&WRS stock now resides on the S&CR. *MJS*

What most people come for – steam and plenty of it! Blunsdon station is seen in all its glory on 5 June 1993, as *Richard Trevithick* blows off, while Haydn Roberts gazes trackwards from the cab and, on the platform, two onlookers scratch their heads in tandem. Elsewhere, blue skies, green leaves, the brightly painted ex-Claydon Junction, Oxford, signal box and well-turned-out rolling-stock complete an attractive illustration of the S&CR. *Paul Chancellor*

GAZETTEER

The emergence of the M&SWJR was the result of a long-held desire to see a railway linking Manchester in the north with Southampton in the south, providing an arterial route for the movement primarily of freight traffic. Various schemes were hatched, but many were quickly dispatched by the GWR, who did not look kindly on any interlopers in its sphere of influence, especially bringing standard gauge to its broad gauge domain. But, like King Canute, even the mighty GWR could not stop the tide for ever.

Swindon, Marlborough & Andover Railway

The genesis of the first line over the eventual route was the opening of the Marlborough Railway from Savernake to the market town on 14 April 1864, and the Andover & Redbridge Railway on 6 March 1865. These became the spur that eventually forged a route north from Southampton, by in turn linking Andover and Savernake and Marlborough and Swindon. Between Savernake and Marlborough, the pernicious and obstructive behaviour of the GWR caused the building of an alternative line, the Marlborough & Grafton Railway, in 1898. The original plans were for a 773-yard tunnel at Swindon, from the Town station to a point east of the GWR's Junction station, but after the contractor's money ran out new thoughts were eventually given to diverting east around the hill in the upper part of the town to eventually reach the GWR west of Junction station, at a place called Rushey Platt, in 1881. Even when the new railway reached Swindon, however, the GWR eschewed the opportunity of reaping revenue from accommodating it into a north-south trunk route, choosing instead to continue its obstructiveness. This brought the Swindon & Cheltenham Extension Railway into being, opening for freight traffic on 1 November 1883, and giving the new line access on its own metals as far north as Andoversford, just south of Cheltenham. Here, tracks were shared with the GWR's route from Banbury – needless to say, there was again a certain lack of co-operation from the mightier organisation. The Midland Railway (at the northern end) and the London & South Western Railway (at the southern) enjoyed cordial relations and had a common enemy – the GWR. This led to the formation of the...

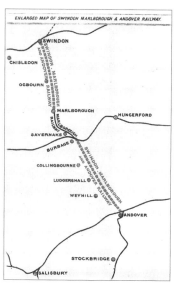

Midland & South Western Junction Railway

Not least due to the machinations of the GWR – in addition to the heavy expense in constructing the northern end of the route – the new railway, formed under an Act of 23 June 1884, was immediately in grave financial trouble, and it took the wizardry of Sam Fay, assuming the role of General Manager from 1 February 1892, to wrest it out of the hands of the Receiver, achieved on 27 May 1897. Freight was attracted in

A contemporary map showing how the two sections of the Swindon, Marlborough & Andover Railway, opened in 1882 and 1884, were linked by the earlier Marlborough Railway of 1864. The SM&AR became part of the newly amalgamated M&SWJR in 1884.

126

any way possible, even including beer trains to the south from Burton-on-Trent, and during the two World Wars it became a vital passage for troop trains, ambulance trains and those shifting massive quantities of war materials. Indeed, at times during the Second War the route was jammed with traffic, all stations and loops being occupied for hours on end with coal, freight and military trains – all in addition to normal traffic! Investment in infrastructure improvements flowed from this, but these were never to reap real benefit after the war, as passenger flows were never heavy and both the absorption by the GWR in 1923 and British Railways in 1948 saw the route relegated under normal conditions to just another country branch. When BR cut passenger services to one train each way between Cheltenham and Andover from 30 June 1958, then diverted passenger trains from Cheltenham (Lansdown) to St James station in November of the same year, it was effectively finished as a through route. Passenger services were finally withdrawn on 11 September 1961, followed by freight for the majority of the route within three years, thereby ending the 80-year struggle.

Swindon & Cricklade Railway

Born in 1978, from an idea of restoring a stretch of the old railway, initially from Swindon Town station towards Marlborough, the disparate parties were eventually brought together by Martin Smith. At the time rails still stretched from Town to Moredon Power Station and to the former GWR main line from Rushey Platt, but these were taken up in the final months of 1978 to enable a new road to be built. The emerging railway was already in discussions with the local Council, but was powerless to stop this bisecting of the old trackbed. A rethink was called for, and focus turned to the run from the Power Station northwards towards Cricklade, but here again there were problems. From Council plans, the railway was aware of projected development in the Moredon area, albeit likely to be 15/20 years hence. Discussions focused on the effects this would have on the S&CR and how they might be overcome, but no satisfactory conclusion was reached, finally persuading the railway, in the autumn of 1978, that they must – reluctantly – accept that the start would have to be at Blunsdon, with plans to run south, rather than the other way round as originally envisaged. On 13 November of that year the Swindon & Cricklade Railway Company Ltd was incorporated and the pace now quickened.

Through the good offices of many local companies, the railway was offered services and items at either reduced prices or no cost at all. Such an offer was the chance to salvage the platform materials from Rushey Platt low-level and Swindon Town stations – not only a useful addition to stock, but, perhaps equally importantly, genuinely 'ex-M&SWJR' in as much as they were from the old line. Similar such 'donations' were the long-term loan of a Fowler 0-4-0 diesel shunter from Coopers (Metals) Ltd, Swindon (early in 1978); all the remaining railway materials – including another diesel shunter – on the closure of W. D. & H. O. Wills's Colbourne Street, Swindon, site in 1980; and a signal box, oil and a myriad of other items, some mentioned in the captions to the photographs – many potentially expensive items.

From these tentative and frequently thwarted beginnings, the railway gradually progressed at Blunsdon, and northwards, to provide rides for the public from 1983 – growing, despite a surprising degree of apathy and ignorance from the inhabitants of nearby Swindon, to become, by the dawn of the new Millennium, one of the expanding number of railway preservation sites throughout the country, providing recreational facilities for the general public, and with the real prospect of longer-term development and potential, proving that this was not just 'boys playing trains'!

2003 sees the 25th anniversary of the formation of the S&CR, the return to steam of No 7903 *Foremarke Hall* and the genuine prospect of, at last, breaking out southwards from Blunsdon, to new pastures and horizons, growth and success. And with a long-term aim of again reaching Cirencester, the M&SWJR will 'breathe' again.

INDEX OF LOCATIONS

BIBLIOGRAPHY

The Midland & South Western Junction Railway Vols 1-3 (Bartholomew/Barnsley)
Swindon's Other Railway (Bridgeman/Barrett/Bird)
Cheltenham to Andover (Mitchell/Smith)
The Midland & South Western Junction Railway (Bridgeman/Barnsley)
The Midland & South Western Junction Railway (Maggs)
A M&SWJR Album (Barrett/Bridgeman/Bird)
Discovering Lost Railways (Cockman)
British Railways Locomotive Stock Changes & Withdrawal Dates Vols 1, 2, 3, 5 & 6 (McManus)
Various issues of *Tiddley Dyke*
Various issues of *Railway Magazine, Railway World*, and *Steam Railway*